Paul Ricoeur

Political
and Social Essays

Collected and Edited by
David Stewart and Joseph Bien

Ohio University Press, Athens

ACKNOWLEDGMENTS

The editors wish to thank the following journals and publishing houses for graciously granting permission to translate and include in this anthology the essays by Paul Ricoeur, which are numbered to correspond with the Table of Contents.

1. "Nature et liberté," in *Existence et nature*, edited by Ferdinand Alquie (Paris: Presses Universitaires de France, 1962), pp. 125-137.
2. "A Critique of B. F. Skinner's *Beyond Freedom and Dignity*," *Philosophy Today*, 17 (Summer, 1973), pp. 166-175.
3. "Que signifie 'humanisme'?" *Comprendre: Revue de la société Européene de Culture*, 15 (1956), pp. 84-92.
4. "Violence et langage," in number 59 of *Recherches et Débats: La violence* (Paris: Desclée de Brouwer, 1967), pp. 86-94.
5. "Ye Are the Salt of the Earth," *Ecumenical Review*, 10 (1958), pp. 264-276.
6. "Faith and Culture," *The Student World*, 50 (1957), pp. 246-251.
7. "De la nation à l'humanité: tâche des chrétiens," *Le Christianisme social*, 73 (1965), pp. 493-512.

8. "Le Projet d'une morale sociale," *Le Christianisme social*, 74 (1966), pp. 285-295.
9. "Urbanisation et secularisation," *Le Christianisme social*, 74 (1967), pp. 327-341.
10. "Les Adventures de l'état et la tâche des chrétiens," *Le Christianisme social*, 66 (1958), pp. 452-463.
11. "Du Marxisme au communisme contemporain," *Le Christianisme social*, 67 (1959), pp. 151-159.
12. "Le Socialisme aujourd'hui," *Le Christianisme social*, 69 (1961), pp. 451-460.
13. "Ethics and Culture," *Philosophy Today*, 17, (Summer, 1973), pp. 153-165.
14. "Taches de l'éducateur politique," *Esprit*, 33 (1965), pp. 78-93.

Appreciation is also gratefully extended to the following translators: Donald Siewert, David Pellauer, Hoke Robinson, Michael Gordy, Kirk Augustine, and Françoise Bien. Their co-operation and continued interest in the project is in large part responsible for the existence of this collection. Appreciation is also expressed to James Boyse, whose many suggestions proved invaluable, and most of all to Paul Ricoeur, whose support has been a source of constant encouragement.

CONTENTS

T HE ARTICLES IN THIS COLLECTION, WHICH WERE ORIGI-
nally addressed to a European audience, nevertheless reflect concerns that I am convinced have a global
importance. I am more and more coming to see that
the emergence of a single, world-wide civilization,
with the problems that this poses, constitutes one of
the most important concerns for reasoned reflection.
To recapture the full range of the meaning of our
humanity and to open up the maximum number of
possibilities for every person, is a challenge for thinkers
in every human discipline. The divergencies of our
economic and political systems should not be seen as
a threat but as a locus for an expanding and continuing
dialogue on basic human issues.

I hope that the appearance of these essays in English
will contribute to such a dialogue, and I wish to express
my thanks to the editors and translators for making
these materials available to a wider American audience.

Paul Ricoeur

Editors' Introduction

THIS COLLECTION OF ESSAYS ON POLITICAL AND SOCIAL themes is a supplement to an earlier anthology, *History and Truth*, first published in 1954 and revised and enlarged in 1964 (English translation, 1965).[1] That series of articles showed the social and political concerns that were in the background of Ricoeur's work from the very beginning. In the Preface to the first edition, Ricoeur mentioned four interests in his life: university teacher, student of the history of philosophy, member of the *Esprit* editorial staff, and listener to the Christain message. Whereas *History and Truth* highlighted the first two of these interests, this collection of later essays shows the equal effect of the latter two interests on Ricoeur's work. The personalistic movement founded by Emmanuel Mounier, whose journal *Esprit* provides a continuing forum for the discussion of social questions, continues to be a dominant interest in Ricoeur's life. And Ricoeur's commitment to the Christian faith is evident in

1

virtually every analysis he offers of the social and political problems confronting modern man.

Ricoeur is perhaps best known for his massive *Philosophie de la volonté*, which begins with a phenomenological analysis of volition and leads, by way of a philosophical anthropology, to a recovery of the religious, mythic, and poetic roots of the human quest for meaningful existence. One who knows this work will not be surprised, then, to see reflected in this collection of essays Ricoeur's deep and lasting commitment both to the significance of the individual and to the religious affirmations of the Christian faith. This collection of articles, which span a decade and a half of Ricoeur's work, gives eloquent testimony to his deeply rooted belief in the efficacy of the word—the spoken word, the written word, and the prophetic word of the Christian Gospel. As he noted in the Preface to *History and Truth*: "As a member of the team of *Esprit*, I believe in the efficacity of speech which thoughtfully elucidates the generating themes of an advancing civilization. As a listener to the Christian message, I believe that words may change the 'heart,' that is, the refulgent core of our preferences and the positions which we embrace."[2]

Ricoeur's two concerns for promoting the significance of the individual and for the redemptive power of the Christian Gospel are related, as his essay entitled "What Does Humanism Mean?" makes abundantly clear. For any humanism worthy of the name, by which Ricoeur understands the wager that man can act efficaciously in the world, is predicated on the affirmation that man is *only* man: no longer

Nietzsche's "human, all too human," but "human, *only* human" is the guiding theme of Ricoeur's analysis of man in society. Whereas some representatives of contemporary French philosophy—most notably Sartre—explicitly assert that man's continually unfulfilled task is to become God, Ricoeur insists on the contrary that man is only man when he recognizes that he is not God, and the thrust of Ricoeur's analysis is to show the futility of the human enterprise to become God. Whether it be the divinization of man by man or the call for ultimate commitment made by political ideologies, the final result of man's refusal to recognize his own humanity is the appearance of the demonic in the world.

But what are the "generating themes" of civilization today to which Ricoeur also refers in his autobiographical reflection? There are many, as the essays in this collection show, but two stand out in particular: the emergence of a world-wide civilization, and the diminution of the individual faced with the overwhelming complexity of the economic, technological, and political forces that shape our lives. How can the individual exert effective action in a world dominated by multi-national corporations, militant ideologies, and immense bureaucracies the reality of which would not even seem appropriate in a Kafka nightmare? To pose the problem more specifically, what is the role of the Christian in such a world? Ricoeur rejects the easy answer that would relegate the Christian to a role exclusively dominated by private piety, personal salvation, and prayer. Piety and social commitment are not opposite poles on a continuum but are concomitant responsibilities for the Christian. "It would be a complete mistake," Ricoeur insists in the essay entitled "Ye Are the Salt of the Earth," that "it would be a complete mistake to regard personal piety and commitment within the church as opposed to commitment in the world."[3]

But if the role of the Christian intellectual in shaping human destiny comes down to the power of the word, the power of speech, how is this power to be inserted effectively into the world of politics, economics, and culture? To be sure, this century has seen too much of useless rhetoric and empty sloganeering. What is needed for effective action in the social and political arena is expertise as well as dedication. The Christian committed to effective social action must equip himself with all the tools that technological society offers him. But in directing this expertise, coupled with the redemptive and reconciling power of the word, the activist must not be seduced into an effete reaction *against* the large bureaucracies or the impersonal organizations that dominate twentieth-century life. The redemptive power of the Christian word of reconciliation must not be directed, Quixote-like, against politics, which is not inherently evil, or against the institutions or the "establishment" which are so frequently singled out as villains. In the same essay Ricoeur argues that "the message of love must be transmitted through the modern channels offered by the world as it is; it must not lose itself in vague regrets or protests against the rules of the game."[4]

Behind the façade of the problems confronting modern man, Ricoeur sees, at a deeper level, the problem of values. The most basic value—that of

4

the meaning of human life itself—gets shunted aside by the demands of a consumer-oriented society, a society in which man is valuated primarily by his work and his consumption. In the face of this, the dominant task of the Christian committed to redemptive social action is to reaffirm the value of the person. This affirmation takes many forms—such as the task of democratizing economic planning, redistributing the available resources to create a better life for the have-nots, and shattering all ideologies, whether they be political, scientific, or religious.

But the overwhelming fact about contemporary man is that he is indisputably a citizen of the world. In an era when electronic communication presents us with a shrunken world, and at a time when diverse cultures are meeting and melding, it is necessary that man see himself not as a member of an isolated culture or a single nation-state but rather as a member of a single, world-wide humanity. "We are certainly the first historical epoch," Ricoeur observes, "which takes a global view of its destiny."[5] It is as reinforcement of this fact that the affirmations of the Christian faith can take hold, for the Christian view of man is that of a single humanity. This world-wide view of humanity, or the mondialization of the word, as Ricoeur refers to it, is most sharply focused in the figure of Christ and in the Cross, which confronts man with this fact: The Cross is not an isolated event but an event with world-wide significance. St. Paul proclaimed that in Christ there is neither Jew nor Greek, slave nor freedman, male nor female (Galatians 3:28), and the Cross signifies that humanity must now be seen as "man complete, man indivisible, beyond all political particularism."[6]

Even when armed with the Christian view of man, the Christian must act as an individual, for there is no "Christian" politics, Ricoeur insists, but only the politics of the Christian as a citizen acting efficaciously in the world. To be sure, such action implies a tension at the very heart of the Christian message of redemption and reconciliation. The Christian is torn between two demands—the ethic of an absolute love, on the one hand, and the ethic of expedient action in the world on the other. Effective action in the world of politics, economics, or social planning may call for a kind of compromise between the two demands. Ricoeur poses the problem in these terms: "The religious conscience says: 'If thou art not perfect in every respect, thou art not perfect at all.' Politics is never subject to this law; its achievements can never be more than relatively good."[7] How, then, is the Christian committed to effective social action to resolve this dilemma?

Ricoeur is close to the American theologian, Reinhold Niebuhr, when he answers that effective social action must be willing to take the risk of accomplishing a limited good. Rejected are the extremes—a utopian piety unconcerned with the problems of society, and a militant religious fanatacism which resolves such problems in terms of absolutes. The Christian can never resolve the tension between the demand for absolute perfection and the demand for the achievement of a limited and relative good; he lives continually within this tension, and he must keep this tension alive. The problem for the Christian involved in social action is no longer that of "maintaining . his innocence, but that of *limiting his culpability.*"[8] And it is at this point that the Christian's commitment to effective action in the world is bolstered by the Christian affirmation of forgiveness and grace.

But at the same time, the Christian is a profaner of ideologies, a smasher of idolatrous pretensions to totality. Here again Ricoeur introduces a biblical note: the eschatological emphasis of Christian Scripture gives both a meaning and a limit to human history. It provides meaning in the sense that man is an actor in a cosmic drama in which, nourished by his creaturely distance from God, he functions in an efficacious role. But the biblical themes of the Day of Judgment, the Day of the Lord, the End of history, or the Last Day, introduce a provisional note into all human enterprises. Not only do these themes signify that all human history is enacted under the judgment of God, they also indicate that no human solution is ever final. All nations, states, civilizations, and cultures are only provisional, and no social institution can ever be the embodiment of absolute good.

These eschatological themes also reinforce the Christian's commitment to efficacious social action in another way, for they provide a workable view of the State as both a promise and a threat. Even a cursory reading of history makes clear that the State, more often than not, has been the embodiment of the demonic forces unleashed in society. And it is not by accident that Christian Scripture, in the

7

book of Revelation, describes the State as the great
beast. But St. Paul also acknowledges the redemptive
power of the State, its function of introducing order
and justice into human society. It is this dual
reading of the State that sees it as fulfilling a
legitimate function, but a function that is always
provisional and incomplete. "This double theological
pattern is full of meaning for us," Ricoeur insists.
"We henceforth know that it is not possible to adopt
for ourselves either a religiously motivated anarchism
under the pretext that the State does not confess
Jesus Christ, or an apology for the State in the name
of 'Be obedient to the authorities.' The State *is* this
dual-natured reality, simultaneously instituted and
fallen."[9]

Whereas Ricoeur's earliest discussions of the
threat posed by modern ideologies were written with
vivid memories of Hitlerism (Ricoeur was himself
a prisoner of the Germans during World War II),
this collection of essays reflects the more immediate concerns of Stalinism, the Algerian war,
France's Indo-China conflict, and America's involvement in Viet Nam. But although the theaters
have changed, Ricoeur sees the same basic problem
emerging—the problem of political power, which
can only be resolved by a new vision of man.[10]
Essential to his new vision of man is the role of
the intellectual who, by preserving as well as re-
newing man's cultural heritage, calls man toward
the future while simultaneously re-rooting him in
the past. No function is more important during this
period of the emergence of a single, universal
civilization. For technology, unlike esthetic and

literary creativity, is without a past, and the developing nations face the threat of losing their past in the overwhelming development of a technological, consumer-oriented society. The task of the educator today, as Ricoeur sees it, is to be animated by the twin temporalities of past and future. We only have a cultural personality, Ricoeur insists, "to the extent that we entirely assume our past, its values and its symbols, and are capable of reinterpreting it totally."[11]

Faced with the complexities of contemporary society, man must not fall back upon the simplistic yearning for an uncomplicated past. But neither does Ricoeur counsel an easy and optimistic doctrine of progress. The events of the first half of this century belie such a naïve alternative. The present situation does not call for pessimism or negation; both responses would be a retreat from the cultural heritage of the West which was sustained by the ongoing task of creating civilization. That is the role of the humanist today, and in this he is nourished by the Christian confidence in man's future, for "the first sign of Christian hope is to believe that something can always be done in every situation."[12] But humanism makes sense only if man is free to shape his culture and his society, and it is therefore not surprising to find human freedom running as a contrapuntal theme throughout all of these essays. Human freedom, however, is not absolute, and it is constantly mediated by society's institutions—the church, the business organization, and perhaps most forcibly of all, the State. For it is the State, in the final analysis, that stands both

9

as a continual threat to free and efficacious action but also as the means by which such actions are extended to society as a whole.

Ricoeur's concern with the articulation of the view that the State allows the expression and development of individual freedom through and by societal institutions must be seen as an extension of his lifelong endeavor to integrate and explicate the concept of freedom as it is both embodied and attenuated in man's social activities. For Ricoeur freedom can be reduced neither to a Kantian concept of autonomy nor to a positivistic variant of external actualization; it is rather to be understood as partaking to a certain extent of both notions: it is consequently both more and less than either.

The key to the understanding of Ricoeur's notion of freedom lies in an appreciation of the reasoning behind his dialectical juxtaposition of nature and freedom. Nature is seen to be simultaneously freedom's other, and its most primary, mediation. If freedom is understood as potency to act, one can understand the "mark of freedom" to be the characteristic seal of the products of human activity. And it is these external products which limit, but at the same time allow for and direct, man's potential freedom within the world of social activity. Freedom can thus be understood to have a "history," in the Hegelian sense of an actualization. Nature and freedom, which at first appear as opposites, are understood finally to be complementary; it is from the mediation of freedom and primitive nature that what one might call a second nature, a cultural or human nature, appears. This second nature must be under-

10

stood neither as a simple mute product or object, for this would lead us into a hopeless dichotomy within the realm of action, nor as a reduction of action to habit, although habit does play an auxiliary role in any notion of social action. This second nature might be thought of as a chronometer serving both as the medium in which men act and as the measure by which all are judged. In such a manner one may speak of individual freedom while never losing the general notion of human freedom. The history of freedom is necessarily open-ended, for if one were to speak of a closing or final moment of history, it would be either to deny freedom its potency of expression by eliminating its natural expressions in action, or to reduce it to mere external behavior as Skinner seems to do in such works as *Beyond Freedom and Dignity.*

In his position on the editorial board of *Esprit* and as a frequent contributor to such journals as *Le Christianisme social,* Ricoeur has attempted, as a Christian and as a philosopher, to confront the political and social problems facing modern man. Two related sets of problems are seen as especially critical: (1) the change from the national or regional allegiances of preceding centuries to the twentieth-century realization of world dependency based on modern technology, with the associated economic and political practices; and (2) the resultant move to the ever greater levels of abstraction exemplified by bureaucracy and social and economic planning; with the attendant diminishing of the active role and importance of the individual. Here again Ricoeur's approach is by means of a sort of hermeneutical dialectic. Taking initially two supposedly opposing concepts, violence and non-violence, he finds through a series of mediations not simple opposition but degrees of difference and stages of understanding; and without denying the necessity of either concept, he arrives at a notion of dialogue in which can be found the realization of both and a move towards rational meaning.

> Step by step everything political is touched by the turgid play of meaning and violence. And undoubtedly we should speak first of meaning, for politics exists because the city exists—therefore because individuals have begun and partly succeeded in overcoming their private violence by subordinating it to a rule of law. The words of the city bear this universal mark, which is a kind of non-violence. But at the same time the community is politically united only because a force voices this form and communicates to the social body the unity of a will which makes decisions and imposes them in order to render them enforceable. Yet this great will, which is the law for individuals, is at the same time like a great irascible individual who at times speaks the language of fear, of anger, of offended dignity, of impudent boasting, that is to say, of violence. Thus the rule of law which gives form to the social body is also power, an enormous violence which elbows its way through our private violences and speaks the language of value and honor."[13]

Violence is embedded in the very action of man and should not in all circumstances be seen as evil; nor should non-violence always be the manner of man's action. There is the natural violence of the surging river or the volcano, just as there may be violent defense of country by exploited peoples throughout the world. This latter violence is not to

12

be judged and employed for its own sake, but rather only in terms of two forms of morality: "To recognize violence where it is, even to have recourse to violence when it is necessary, does not exclude the recognition of the place of the testimony of the non-violent man in history, for if non-violence alone belongs to the morality of conviction, on the other hand the morality of conviction can never take the place of the morality of responsibility."[14] There can never be a final resolution between these two moralities, for Christian humanism shows us that man is neither God nor on the way to being God. He is "only human," a limited creature continually torn between his ideals of perfection and the need for relatively correct action in his social existence. What Ricoeur is calling for, in short, is a new understanding of man that can serve as the basis for social action in the twentieth century.

In his pursuit of such an understanding, it is not surprising that Ricoeur, living in a country where twenty-five percent of the electorate votes communist and many others vote for some form of modified socialism, has had an abiding interest in the claims of Marxism. With the conception of human nature that emerges from the writings of the early Marx, coupled with its further examinations of labor and its analyses of the class struggle, Marxism has attempted to give a global explanation of human relationships. Marx's materialism must, however, be distinguished from crude materialism, and Ricoeur finds the former to be a form of realism in which labor is more than a simple economic category. "That man is a 'producer' emphasizes that he is not nature or animality; moreover he does not 'produce' only to live, but to humanize himself and to humanize nature. Nature itself appears as the 'inorganic body of man.' . . . That is why man's alienation is itself always more than economic: it is the over-all dehumanization of man."[15] In a sort of dialectical genesis Marxism describes man's move from primitive communism to capitalism's economic alienations and beyond to the hoped-for future freedom of communist society. Today man's labor, which could not only satisfy his physical needs but actually realize his true humanity, is reduced to the role of a mere commodity in a market economy and loses its liberating function. Attacks on private property and on money will be essential ingredients in the proletarian revolution that will finally allow man to express himself fully as human being. Marx's call for future revolution is a human but not a moral prescription. It is to be realized through an unfolding of history, rather than by the revolt of a moral conscience. Marx leaves us in the ambiguous position of creating ourselves but only being able to be freed through the process of history. At best this is an ambiguous notion of humanism, Ricoeur finds, and at worst it leads back to a form of mechanistic or crude materialism. At the very least the notion of the individual is lost, for alienation and exploitation cannot be reduced to "individual violences" but must be seen as part of a necessary process.

In *State and Revolution* Lenin had attempted to resolve this ambiguity, but in the process he reduced Marxism to a form of scientistic positivism. Emphasizing a theme that is to be found in Marx—the

State as nothing more than the ruling class' tool for the control of civil society—Lenin stressed the need for the proletariat once in power to oppress all other groups and classes in order to arrive at the final freedom: communist society. He also developed his notion of the party, which was to aid the class and to guide it once in power. It was the party that was simultaneously to instruct the proletariat, to direct its State to final freedom, and, by mediating between the proletariat and history, to replace the notion of the individual lost to Marxism with a special group that, although not adequately grounded in theory, would nonetheless be able somehow to read the movement of history in praxis. Ricoeur sees the result of this notion of the party as the establishment of a particular perspective (the party's) as the sole true insight into the totality of history. Particularity has been enshrined as absolute, and with its mutation the hope for a true humanism has been shut off in the present world situation. Marxism, which claimed to do away with ideology, has been reduced to dogma; it may at some future time become open to the promises of freedom it first expressed, but the party's "progress" from Lenin to Stalin to the neo-Stalinists makes this quite remote.

Whereas communism is thus not the solution to guarding the value of the individual in twentieth-century societies, some form of planning and proletarian mass organization is necessary, that is to say, some form of socialism: " . . . socialism is the system in which workers are the dominant social category; it is the system in which a democracy of labor exists side-by-side with planning."[16] Yet while socialism is the most positive alternative to highly developed capitalism, it too poses dangers to individual freedom. By the very fact that socialism attempts to move beyond the motive of the maximization of profits to the recognition of a hierarchy of needs, it necessitates the "socialization" of property and the development of ever greater and more intricate organs of long-range planning. But this increasing concentration of planning power inevitably conflicts with the other ideal of socialism: the democracy of labor. The scope and complexity of the social functions that the State assumes require analytical and technical skills that are not well developed in the citizenry at large, which therefore tends to be reduced to symbolic participation in social decision-making. Ricoeur suggests that only through continual surveillance can socialism herald the end of non-freedom. State organs must be as decentralized as possible, and long-range decision-making must admit a number of levels of "subordinate choices." Without such efforts socialism may well amount to only a more or less benign caricature of the Stalinist party-proletariat relationship.

But there is a second and possibly more serious danger that may result from a successful socialism. The rationality of production may spawn a set of values that all too closely resembles hedonism, as has to a great extent already been witnessed in the Scandinavian countries. Satisfaction might thus come to be understood as simple pleasure, and one might find that "socialism would then only be a more advanced and more rational industrialism pursuing the same dream of the promethean conquest of well-being and of nature. It would only have pursued in a more rational way maste·y of the world by means of a society geared to total satisfaction."[17] If socialism is to avoid this return to narrow utilitarianism, it must remember its true origin as a demand of the underpriviliged. Socialist humanism must be concerned not only with the interests of a given nation, but with the world-wide suffering of mankind. Rather than seeing work as a necessary evil, the *quid pro quo* of leisure, socialists must remember that man expresses himself through his labor everywhere. And it is precisely with this universal concern for his fellowman that the socialist humanist can also pursue the Christian goal of attempting to realize the good in an always imperfect and intractable world situation.

The State is not, in this view, something to be eliminated, as anarchists have advocated. Ricoeur correctly points out that, whereas some of the bourgeois apparatus may disappear, there will always be the need for the social organization that only a State can provide. What he believes is needed in the present era is a strengthening of the State— a strengthening of its authority, not of its power. The establishment of a socialist State that allows for truly human development will demand strong central power, but this power must be divided among the executive, the legislative, and the independent judicial branches of government. So also must the cultural organs—particularly the universities and the media—maintain a complex relationship of partial but not total independence of the State: total subservience to the State would lead directly to tyranny, while total independence of the State would result in dependence on private interests, unrestrained competition and possible self-destruction. Even within the socialist State "we must also continue the task of *liberal* politics, which has always consisted of two things: to divide power among powers, to control executive power by popular representation."[18] The State is the arena in which the citizen continually witnesses the interplay between freedom and order. Neither extreme—freedom understood as anarchy or order understood as tyranny —is to be sought, for it is rather the continual tension between the two that best allows man to realize his humanity within the political sphere. Utopias are not to be realized, for man is only mortal, but they are valuable as models by which one can gauge present political realities and orient his action to bring about a rational State in which the individual's freedom can be taken up and joined with that of his fellowmen in a human dialogue.

NOTES

1. *History and Truth*, trans. Charles A Kelbley (Evanston: Northwestern University Press, 1965).
2. *Ibid.*, p. 5.
3. "Ye Art the Salt of the Earth," p. 124.
4. *Ibid.*, p. 114.
5. "From Nation to Humanity: Task of Christians," p. 135.
6. *Ibid.*, p. 153.
7. "Ye Art the Salt of the Earth," p. 121.
8. *Ibid.*
9. "Adventures of the State and the Task of Christians," p. 203.
10. Ricoeur says elsewhere that the central problem of politics is will, which provides a point of contact between Ricoeur's social and political writings and his phenomenological analysis of volition in *Philosophie de la volunté*. For

Editors' Introduction

an analysis of a similar methodology underlying both of these spheres of Ricoeur's work, see David Stewart, "The Christian and Politics: Reflections on Power in the Thought of Paul Ricoeur," *The Journal of Religion* 52 (No. 1, January, 1972): pp. 56-83.

11. "The Tasks of the Political Educator," p. 292.
12. "Ye Art the Salt of the Earth," p. 113.
13. "Violence and Language," pp. 93-94.
14. *Ibid.*, p. 100.
15. "From Marxism to Contemporary Communism," pp. 220-21.
16. "Socialism Today," p. 237.
17. *Ibid.*, p. 240.
18. "Adventures of the State and the Task of Christians," p. 213.

19

PART I

THE MEANING OF MAN

1

Nature and Freedom

Can we speak of a human nature? The question is a difficult one, for the word "nature" has many meanings. I propose to take as a guide the adventures of another philosophical theme, freedom. It is indeed remarkable how both in its formation and in its use the concept of freedom displays in a systematic order most of the diverse meanings of the notion of nature. It is this sequence which we shall try to reconstruct.

In an initial movement of thought, a regressive and reductive analysis, freedom is set in opposition to the whole idea of nature, to both nature in general and to human nature. But this triumph by mere opposition is a Pyrrhic victory, for such freedom is merely possible; to become real it must reaffirm nature both in man and outside him. There is no nature *of* man, we say in the first movement of thought. But there is a nature *in* man, we shall

Translated by Donald Siewert

have to say in accordance with a second movement, which replies to the first with a progressive synthesis of experience. Our ultimate problem, therefore, will be this: How can nature appear in turn as both the "*other*" of freedom *and* as its primordial *mediation*? What is the meaning of nature in general—what *is* nature in general—that it plays this double role with regard to freedom?

We shall thus follow first the regressive route, the denial of nature, and then the synthetic route, the reaffirmation of it, passing through the point where freedom is at its absolute maximum, a point marked by the complete absence of nature.

The Destruction of Nature

This analysis can be divided into three moments which proceed in a sequence that is the reverse of the three degrees of the progressive synthesis.

First Moment

If we want to start not with concepts that come from reflection and philosphical discussion, but with living experience, the very first breach with nature is summed up in the threefold conquest of the institution, the tool, and language. This threefold conquest is that of the humanity of man, and from it a threefold opposition can be established in which the term nature appears each time as the "other" in a pair of meanings.

As opposed to the institution (νόμος, *nomos*), nature appears as a "state"—the state of nature—prior to any law, prior to the civil state properly so called. This state is hidden, suppressed, perhaps even sacrificed through some real or fictitious contract for the sake of the security, order and freedom of the civil (i.e. institutional) state. Nature appears in retrospect as the unchecked reign of passions, fear and violence, as disorder and war.

As for the arts and technology—the second aspect of this conquest of humanity—they reveal a different opposition: that between what is produced by nature (φύσει) and what is produced by art (τέχνη). In this opposition between *artefacta* and *naturalia*, the human order takes on the appearance of an artifice, a Leviathan. Not only tools, but also institutions (which we have already mentioned) and language (of which we have yet to speak) are produced "by art" and not "by nature." Here nature no longer signifies disorder and violence, but spontaneity in the coming into existence, production according to an internal principle. This aspect of nature is supreme in the movements of living things. The *naturalia par excellence* are the *animalia*.

Finally—the third aspect of this prereflective opposition—the world of signs and language makes nature appear to be the pre-existing order of mute expressions and brute appearances. Thus the protagonists in the *Cratylus* could wonder whether words are in conformity with the nature of things (κατὰ φύσιν i.e., κατὰ αυτά τὰ πράγματα). Nature is then the ensemble of things, of bodies, of existents totally opposed to λεκτόν. Nature is that which *is*, pure and simple, as opposed to that which is *said*, as opposed to *discourse*, with its order, its logic and its claim to truth.

Thus as we have progressed in the humanity of man toward *logos*, toward Speech—through *techné* and *nomos*—nature has revealed itself to be, successively, violence in man, spontaneity in living organisms, and mute, brute existence in mere objects. As the circle of nature expanded, the gap widened between humanness and naturalness. Prior to any scholastic discussions, by being bound up with institutions, labor, and discourse, concrete freedom is opposed to this threefold nature. Thus an existence deliberated upon, preferred and chosen, is wrenched from a natural, that is to say an unfree, existence.

Conceived in this way, however, the opposition between nature and freedom remains only partial. Man retains a community of existence and of meaning with nature. He retains it as long as rational life seems to him to accomplish a *télos* which fulfills the appetition he finds in living things and the potency which tends in everything to action, to entelechy. One can even say that there is a human nature co-ordinate with nature, both characterized by inclination toward a perfected existence.

But this connivance, this conspiracy, this connaturality, has been shattered by reflection. We have lost that nature of things and that nature of man. This loss is indeed a meaningful destruction, which belongs henceforth to the exemplary history of freedom. It is this which we shall reconstitute in the second and third moments of our analysis.

Second Moment

The destruction of the concept of nature, as conceived on the model of appetite, is bound up with the scientific act as such. But it remains inoperative without the conclusive destruction of *human* nature, which we shall save for the third stage.

As we know, the mathematization of the real, the formulation of the principle of inertia, the purely experimental conception of the connections among things, have destroyed the idea of productive force or natural potency. They have led to the wholly formal idea of nature as the correlate of possible experience or, in terms of transcendental subjectivity, as the lawfulness of experience itself.

The previous opposition between man and nature is radicalized, although it is not yet total. It is more radical in that, in the first place, the world of inertia and mechanics appears as something pure in relation to the activities of domination, exploitation and possession. In industry the struggle with nature prevails over man's belonging to and participating in nature. The opposition of man to nature appears still more radical in the cosmological antinomy of two kinds of causality: causality through freedom, by which something begins in the world, and natural causality, by which one thing follows upon another according to laws. This antinomic division of causality marks a more decisive break on the speculative level with the ancient vision of the world as a progression of potencies and appetites than the rupture brought about by industry on the pragmatic level. Henceforth every affirmation of man's belonging to nature must be affirmed beyond this antinomy, not in indifference to it.

But the opposition to nature is nevertheless not

yet complete. As long as the idea of human nature has not been called in question, it is possible to imagine a continuity between the immutability of the laws of nature or the transcendental lawfulness of nature and a human order in some sense *analogous* to it. For nature was potency only because the very notion of potency remained related to that of form, of essence, or of *raison d'être*. A concept of nature—of nature as essence—can outlive the concept of nature as desire and force. Consequently it is still possible that relations of perfection, conceived of as the *raison d'être* of the human order, are combined with relations of necessity in a single natural whole. And even if this metaphysics seems impossible after the Kantian revolution, the style of lawfulness, necessity and apriority which determines morality and which permits us to speak of "practical reason" remains homogeneous with the lawfulness of nature and enables us to regard nature as a "type" of morality: "Act as if the maxim of your action could be considered a law of nature." Thus, nature remains the *homologue* of morality so long as the latter is thought of as an order. It is this homology, in the proper sense of the word, which makes us admire in equal measure the law of nature revealed in the heavens and the moral law engraved in our hearts.

Third Moment

The negation of the notion of human nature, therefore, results not only from a critique of the notion of nature in general, but from a critique of the

humanness of man that sets him apart from the
naturalness of nature. This third moment in our
reflection has its condition in the two preceding
moments, but it has another feature specific to
itself which we could call the *exile* of the *Cogito*
whose stages are easily recognized. In distinguishing
"that which depends on us" from "that which does
not depend on us," I become indifferent to all
external order at the same time that I render all
things non-essential. As I withdraw the certitude
of thinking from the region of doubtable things, I
inscribe the very existence of my thought on the
borders of this universe of things. In perceiving
the "I think" as a consciousness which "is able to
accompany all my representations," I place this "I"
outside of the sphere of objectivity. I dissociate it
from the history of the thinker; I refuse to give it
the ontological status of the thinking thing. In short,
when I put into parentheses not only nature itself
(*Naturhaft*) but that which is wholly natural (*natür-
lich*) in the mundane, historical and logical order, I
arrive at an *Ego meditans* which is no longer either
engaged or interested.

Can we go further? Assuredly we can. The destruction of the idea of human nature is fully complete
only when theoretical distance becomes practical
rejection. The idea of nothingness (*néant*), introduced as a gap between the "I" and the sum of its
motivations, is the symbol of the extreme *dena-
turing* to which it is undoubtedly necessary to go
in order to comprehend the problem posed by the
notion of human nature. When I can say, "I am not
that which I am," the rupture between the *quod* of

existence and the *quid* of essence completes the downfall of the last meaning of "nature," that is, the essence, the immutability of the *raison d'être*, the lawfulness of the order. As we know, this final dissolution is the product of a conjunction of the themes of freedom and temporality. If essentiality implies immutability, anything that reveals the historical character of the immutable, any genealogy that restores the process of sedimentation by which meanings, values and truths come to simulate the immobility of things, delivers free existence from the bondage of constituted essence. *Wesen ist gewesen.* The essential is the having been; to know that is to deliver oneself from the prestige of essential nature.

Thus, having withdrawn from things, the *Cogito* now withdraws from that which in itself is a thing. Having absented itself from *nature*, it now absents itself from *its own* nature and, lacking a nature, surrenders itself to the throes of self-determination. A *pure I* is born at the moment when all internal and external nature is negated.

This is the final limit of the reductive analysis and, at the same time, the zero point of nature.

THE REAFFIRMATION OF NATURE

At this culmination of reflection, at this extreme of rejection, it is the most negative, the most unreal, the most impotent of freedoms that we have won. Nothing has so far been done to make freedom something affirmative, real and effective. In the process first of affirming freedom, then of actualizing it, and finally of making it something effective and powerful, a new set of relations between freedom and nature emerges. Let us consider the three moments of this process, which correspond in reverse order to the three moments of our regressive analysis.

First Moment

It appears first that the act of denial, of annihilation, of *néantisation* (or whatever we call it) in which the *Cogito* consumes itself is not yet the positive act, the thetic judgment: I *am*. Perhaps we should venture to say that a philosophy of negation will never be anything but the opposite of a philosophy: its examples are all experiences of crises, of breakdown, indeed of destruction, and they can all be shown to be truncated experiences. I deny my past, a tradition, or a received value only in order to affirm a new value, to start a new tradition, to set out on a new course of existence. Someone who remains at the level of negation remains in the adolescence of freedom. The passage to maturity is the passage to affirmation: I am, that is so, let that be. But if we look for the prejudice implicit in any overemphasis on negation, it is to be found, not in the notion of nothingness, but rather in the notion of being, which is mistakenly identified with things, with inertia, with death. Should we not say: to exist is to act? Does not being, in the first instance, signify an act? But what shields thought from the act of existing is the usurped prominence of essence, which was, as we have seen, the last refuge of the idea of nature. The mistaken quarrel over essence and existence has resulted from this excessive promotion of the idea of essence, wrongly substituted for that of being.

It would be impossible to exaggerate the importance of this point for the rest of our examination of nature. For my part, I think that it is essential to link up again both a long tradition of the act of existing, which culminated, it seems to me, in the Leibnizian notion of appetition and the Spinozistic notion of effort—*conatus*. Being is act before it is essence, because it is effort before it is representation or idea.

It is because this meaning of being was forgotten that we thought that the emergence of freedom out of nothingness had to be opposed to the essential being, the already completed being, the dead being, of things. But negating the thing is only a secondary episode compared to the complete affirmation of the act of existing, of the effort to persist in being that extends over an indefinite duration. This recovery of what I shall call the active meaning of being is the most fundamental condition for a recovery of nature within freedom. The second moment of our progressive synthesis will attest to its fruitfulness.

Second Moment

The freedom achieved by the reduction of the idea of nature is not only negative, but indeed unreal. But the "I am" in its positivity can certify itself only in the becoming-real of freedom. What does this mean, and what does it imply for the problem of nature?

The real meaning of this becoming-real of freedom

depends on a philosophy of action of which the revised idea of being is only the most fundamental
condition. When we try to establish this philosophy,
however, we encounter another prejudice, which is
no longer the reduction of being to essence, but which
stems from the very operations which have permitted
the triumph of the idea of nature as a necessary
order and as lawfulness. The prestige of these operations, to which we alluded in the second moment of
our reflective analysis, is so great that we feel
inclined to construe all reflection on action as such
on the model of a critique of cognitive operations.
This is how the distinction between the *a priori* and
the empirical, fundamental to the critique of knowledge, has been transferred pure and simple into the
sphere of action. From this transfer of the categories
of knowledge into the sphere of action results the
disastrous opposition between the form of rationality
and the matter of desire. This distinction does not
arise in the order of action but has been borrowed
from the operations that constitute truth. For a consideration of action not simply transferred from a
critique of knowlege—even one called a *Critique
of Practical Reason*—for a dialectic originally and
specifically concerned with action itself, the becoming-real of freedom does not consist in giving a
matter to a form or in subsuming the particular
under a rule.

Jean Nabert has described this dialectic, from a
standpoint rather close to that of Fichte with his
thetic judgment, as the *appropriation* by the ego
of a certainty of existing which constitutes the ego,
but of which it is in many ways dispossessed. This

task of appropriation presupposes that the effort which results in our existence is not homogeneous, that it is at once the positing and the differentiation of the self. The equation of effort and desire is, then, after the equation of being and effort, the second fundamental presupposition of a reflection on action.

One might ask what this desire is a desire for. Let us leave this question hanging for the time being and try to understand—staying at the level of maximum generality—that the Spinozistic *conatus* is the same as the Platonic *eros*. The *Symposium* shows well that love is love of something, but of something which it does not possess, which it lacks. Let us not separate this proposition from the one in the *Ethics* according to which every particular thing tends to persevere in being by an effort that expresses the infinite power of God. Effort, in its most basic structure, is the affirmation of being in the lack of being. In this sense we must reject both the wholly positive ontology of Spinoza, who can understand negation only as external destruction (according to the single axiom of book IV of the *Ethics*), and the wholly negative ontology of Sartre, who in symmetric fashion relegates all positivity in being to the exteriority of the thing.

How does this statement of the problem of action prepare for a recovery of nature within freedom? According to the second moment of our regressive analysis, nature is the form of lawfulness to which morality should become analogous and which itself provides a "type" of the moral law. But the nature that is implied by the dialectic proper to action as such is not a form of lawfulness but rather the very power of desire. And this power is not the "other" of freedom but the mediation which its becoming-real demands.

It would be impossible to overemphasize the fact that the exaggeration of the role of moral obligation, of the moral law, is responsible for the obliteration of the basic problem of action. But this exaggeration has subsisted by feeding on the lawfulness which we must demote from the first rank, as we just now had to challenge the primacy of essence in the theory of being, in order to grasp the much more basic relation of nature as desire to will as the determination of a project.

How can we establish this thesis?

The many modern attempts to work out a theory of *motivation* constitute the first contribution to this reflection on the natural mediations of freedom. What we can keep from all these attempts, in spite of their abstract character (which we shall discuss later), is the following: freedom does not consist in some irrational eruption, but reflective choice always follows from some non-reflective movement, some inchoate act, tendency or inclination which deserves the name of spontaneous will or natural freedom. Nabert has said very well that freedom would remain an idea of reflection—and not an experience— if the free act were not itself produced as the effect of a psychological determinism and if it were not thus itself a party to what he called the law of representation. For it is in this way that the free act can justify itself, can declare itself and communicate itself, by means of the linguistic symbols of its motives.

This is, in first approximation, the recovery of nature as desire in freedom as project. We must still acknowledge that every theory of motivation remains abstract and that the phenomenology of the free act remains a kind of didactic fiction. Can we speak of a free act in an isolated instant? Is it not the case, rather, that the degree of a man's freedom can be calculated or imputed only on the basis of the quality or the flow of his whole life, or at least of a period of life that is viewed against the background of an unfolding destiny? Freedom is less the quality of an act than of a "way of life," *a bios*, which does not occur in any single act but expresses itself in the degree of tension and consistency which permeates a course of existence. The consideration of motives is therefore less decisive for our purposes than this power to act with consistency, to bring about a lasting change, a new course of existence. To begin, they say, is difficult; but to continue, to act self-consistently, is even more difficult. This is the profound truth of the ὁμολογουμένως ζῆν of the Stoics, "harmonious living."

But to live harmoniously, to act with consistency or continuity, is to maintain a relation with nature which is exhausted not in the fleeting moment of a desire, but in the stable persistence of character. To act self-consistently is, properly speaking, to habituate freedom, to bring it about that freedom, directing itself, make of itself a nature under the influence of what it has already become and

36

achieved. This self-direction, this *habitus*, this έξις, can be lived in different degrees, either fatalistically or spontaneously. For fate is already a category of freedom, its lowest degree to be sure, but the first concrete form of freedom's becoming-real.

Let us state precisely this relation between freedom and nature. It consists essentially in freedom's power to *contract* habits. What freedom contracts in this way is itself, that is to say, a "my own," a having-been which is a "now having-myself."

The fact that the task of education is to raise this self-direction to the level of a genuine law of development and to bring about a passage from the inevitability of a character to the spontaneity of a personality does not in the least cancel the law of character. Without the *acquired* nature of a character, we would not even be able to set about acquiring a personality.

Nature thus appears to be involved in the movement by which existence "holds on" to its own experience. And this "holding on" is not just memory; it is in the first instance a practical category, a "having" which our "being" establishes as it acts, an acquired set of preferences, a έξις. It follows from this that ethics consists less in providing matter for the empty form of obligation than in expressing and bringing to full bloom the nature of each individual.

Let us pause now at the end of this second stage of our progressive synthesis; it corresponds to the second stage of the regressive analysis, that is, to the reduction of nature, on the level of representation, to a form of lawfulness. The dialectic of action has restored what the critique of knowledge had canceled out: nature as desire.

Our master in all this is Ravaisson. No one has better understood that the actualization of freedom consists of a double movement: the naturalizing of freedom and the interiorizing of nature. It matters little that Ravaisson thought that habit was the only place where the intersection of the two movements is visible. We shall see in the third moment of our synthesis that this is not the case. Ravaisson at least touches on the essence of the matter when he suggests that nature is not in the first instance a resistance to be overcome, but a tendency to be taken up.[1] More precisely, his idea that there is an infinite approximation of nature by habit as the latter "redescends the spiral" leading back to nature[2] is an extraordinary insight, the fruitfulness of which will appear later on in other connections. Generalizing upon his discovery, Ravaisson writes magnificently: "In all things, the necessity of nature is the warp on which freedom weaves. But it is a living and moving warp, being the necessity of desire, love and grace."[3]

Third Moment

Let us take a third step on the road of this progressive synthesis. It will lead us to the level of the first stage of the regressive analysis, which consists, we recall, in the opposition between the human act of culture and nature considered as violence in man, spontaneity in living organisms and mute existence in mere things. It is this primordial opposition which we must now challenge.

The consideration that follows will help us establish the prevalence of the point of view of mediation over that of opposition. What are we actually looking for in this third moment? To pursue all the way to the end the idea of *real* freedom. But if the dialectic of action is to develop categories proper to itself and not be carried on simply in terms of categories transferred from knowledge, the real in the order of action is not the being-there of fact, which goes along with essence and with possibility conceived simply as such. In the order of action, reality signifies potency, δύναμις, *virtus*. Not potency in the sense of tendency to form, but potency in the sense of operation, effectiveness, expansiveness of action, as political philosophy has generally better understood than moral philosophy, which has been overanxious to exorcise unholy desires.

But how does freedom express its potency?

This question leads us to consider the central dialectic of action, the dialectic of the action and of the work. The mark of freedom upon the world is those lasting objects which cannot be understood except as products of human activity. These objects —which well deserve to be known as "works"— form in turn a context for behavior. We hardly do anything except in the midst of such products of human activity, to the point where things are for the most part, in the etymological sense of the word, *pragmata*. This density of human works is the condensation of my potency; it represents the most complete transaction between the inwardness of effort and the external character of nature.

In an earlier conference we meditated on this law of the work, and I for my part insisted on the *discipline of the finite* which human genius submits to when it grapples with the harsh reality of the work. We have come to the point where the two themes of freedom and nature intersect. We shall not pause today over the *limitation* of human infinity by the work, but over the *naturalizing* of freedom which this discipline of the work implies. We shall say, then, that freedom is potency only by means of a fundamental objectification in works. As long as we do not enter upon this movement of objectification, the theory of freedom remains abstract, as we already said about the phenomenology of the degress of freedom in character and personality. Both of the phenomenologies ignore the function of the work as the intermediary by which freedom appears in the world. Only the consideration of works definitively distinguishes the reflective method from every kind of introspection, by insisting on this detour through the specific objects of our potency for existing.

This is not the place to develop this theory of the works of human potency. In *Fallible Man* I showed that we must turn to the distinction among the spheres of economics, politics, and culture in the exact sense of the word in order to account for the properly human sentiments bound up with the specific objects of each of these spheres. I also attempted, on the basis of these three cycles of objectivity, to reconstitute the Kantian trilogy of the sentiments and passions of having, power and will—of possession, domination and reputation. Here I presuppose this analysis and will not reproduce the argument for it. Instead, I shall go straight to the difficulty it inevitably leads to.

The difficulty is as follows. To what extent do these works of man, these cultural objects which provide a point of support for human desire and which constitute it as human, deserve to be called "natural" mediations? The desirability attributed to the economic object, the desire and the fear occasioned by political power, the sentiments bound up with cultural objects—books, art works, monuments—are these still "natural"? Do we not fall back into the initial opposition between human artifice and nature at the very moment we think we have brought about the naturalization of freedom? In short, must we not admit that nature is forever hidden, buried, lost?

This is a strong objection. But it does not require us to refuse to recognize something natural in the movement of embodiment of our potency for existence. It inclines us to think, rather, that the dialectic of nature and freedom has shifted to the very heart of the cultural object, as is shown by the *desire* and the properly human sentiment in which cultural objects are reflected and interiorized. The cultural object, in fact, has two faces and is open to a double reading. On the one hand, it is always possible to trace out a "genesis" of the desires which support the cultural world, beginning with concealed impulses and ending with the *Will to Power* or with the *libido*. A Nietzschean "genealogy of morals" or a Freudian "psychoanalysis of culture" are not only possible but legitimate. They show that culture cannot be treated as a pure *artifact* without becoming unintelligible. It is always possible to transcribe the acquisition of civilization as a balance between the satisfactions offered and the sacrifices inflicted upon the impulse to life, and even to uncover an impulse to death at the bottom of all of "civilization's discontents." Whether we speak in terms of *ressentiment* or of "sublimation," this genesis of the cultural object takes us back, through transmutation and transvaluation, to the basic impulse "invested" in apparently the most artificial works of man. Far from being unprecedented, these attempts of Freud and Nietzsche are an extension of the Spinozistic treatise on the passions. Spinoza was the first to see that desire and fear, of which all the passions are modulations, derive from the human *conatus* and constitute in their turn the motivating force of all economic, political and cultural acts. A comparison of the *Theologico-Political Treatise* and the *Political Treatise* on the one hand with books III and IV of the *Ethics* on the other will show sufficiently well this rooting of all *artifacts* in the natural potency of man and of things.

But this first reading calls for another. No "genealogy of morals," no "psychoanalysis of culture" can serve as the foundation of an economics, a politics or a culture. The affective genesis is one thing, the origin of their meaning is another. The fact that one and the same *energy* underlies human desire and extends itself continually until it becomes unrecognizable under the masks of civility and morality does not mean at all that economic, political and cultural objects, taken as such, do not have a different history, one more like a Hegelian *Phenomenology of Mind* than a Darwinian genesis. Two histories intersect in the cultural object, the ascending genesis of *libido*, of the *Wille zur Macht*, and the descending genesis of freedom objectifying itself in works. To comprehend the humanity of man would be to comprehend this articulation between the two movements of "sublimation" of impulse in a culture and "alienation" of spirit in a nature.

We have come again, at the end of this sketch, to the theme of Ravaisson, but without the limitation imposed by the theme of habit. Let us repeat one last time with him: "In all things the necessity of nature is the warp on which freedom weaves. But it is a living and moving warp, being the necessity of desire, love and grace."

Conclusion

We asked in the beginning how nature can appear in turn both as the *other* of freedom and as its primordial *mediation*. What is the meaning of nature in general—what *is* nature in general—that it plays this double role with respect to freedom?

The confrontation of the two opposed movements of our meditation permits us to say this:

The relation of mediation between freedom and nature is more fundamental than the relation of opposition. Every other answer to the question of the relation between them deals only with a truncated freedom which exhausts itself in denying an inert nature. Our reflection makes room for an affirma-

43

tive, real and potent freedom which fulfills a living nature.

If it is true that the critique of knowledge excludes from the scientific view of the world the notions of force and desire and reduces the idea of nature to that of lawfulness of experience, reflection on action—irreducible to any critique of knowledge— restores the idea of natural potency as a practical category. This reflection reaches a deeper onto- logical level than theoretical representation, if it is true that being itself signifies act, effort, potency.

The successive mediations of freedom—in a self- consistent sequence of motivation, in the levels of personalization, in the works of culture—constitute a kind of indefinite approximation to the forgotten nature. We say of these mediations what Ravaisson said of habit: together they "can be considered as a method, as the only real method, for the approxima- tion by a continuous infinite convergence of the relation, real in itself but incommensurable so far as our understanding is concerned, between nature and the will."[4]

Yes, it can be admitted that nature is hidden, buried, lost. And nevertheless we must say, again with Ravaisson, that habit—let us say the life of culture—"is an acquired nature, a second nature, which has its fundamental reason in primitive nature but which alone explains primitive nature to the understanding. It is, in short, a natured nature, the work and successive revelation of naturing nature."[5] If we take these statements of Ravaisson seriously, we must say this: It is far from true that the reign of freedom has abolished nature. The second nature

Nature and Freedom

which this reign establishes is the only approximation of the first nature. Nature still speaks in at least one place, in the darkness of the desire which the grand human artifice reveals, that is to say at the same time *manifests* and *conceals*.

Paul Ricoeur, "Nature et liberté," from the collection entitled *Existence et nature*, edited by Ferdinand Alquie (Paris: Presses Universitaires de France, 1962), pp. 125-137.

NOTES

1. Ravaisson, *De l'habitude*, p. 41.
2. *Ibid.*, p. 38.
3. *Ibid.*, p. 57.
4. *Ibid.*, p. 38.
5. *Ibid.*, pp. 38-39.

2

A Critique of B. F. Skinner's
Beyond Freedom and Dignity

The general mood of my approach to Professor Skinner's book is a mixture of disagreement at the level of theory and agreement at a practical level. I, too, feel no great sympathy for some of the things with which he disagrees under the title of the literature of freedom and dignity, that is, arguments for freedom without norms or institutions. I also feel some sympathy for the idea that it might be the task of a technology of behavior to change and improve the "contingencies" of human behavior, thanks to a better knowledge of how they work. But I do not think that the foundations are sound for either the critique of "wild" freedom or the positive programs with which I can agree.

I shall therefore try to indicate how I join partial agreement about the consequences with disagreement about basic concepts.

Translated by David Pellauer

B. F. *Skinner's* Beyond Freedom and Dignity

What disturbs me is the sort of alternative on which the book is built: *either* a technique which works on the contingencies operative on human behavior *or* the naïve claims of autonomous man. I do not think that this alternative is correctly constructed. If Professor Skinner knows perfectly well what he means by behavior, behavioral science, and a technology of behavior—all of which I take for granted—he does not know what he means by "autonomous man." This pseudo-concept is a polemical fiction issuing from the confusion of several levels which I shall try to disentangle in order to identify the points where I agree and where I disagree.

On the first level *autonomous man* refers to "mentalist" psychology, i.e., the claim to build a knowledge of man on the assumption of "mental states" accessible to inner perception. My first point will be that ethical and political issues require a kind of *theory of action* which can bypass this alternative of "mentalism" and "behaviorism."

On a second level *autonomous man* refers to "wild" freedom, i.e., the claim to achieve human freedom without any kind of control, the claim to achieve freedom against institutions. An important part of what Professor Skinner calls the "literature of freedom and dignity" concerns this concept of wild freedom, but this concept does not belong to the same universe of discourse as "mentalism" which is a psychological concept. Rather what is implied at this level is an ethical and political concept of freedom, which I do not think a mere behavioral science is well equipped to deal with.

A technology of behavior may become a part of what I call a politics of freedom, but the main concepts escape the competence of the psychologist. The real issues concern the relation between *freedom and institutions* and the positive aspects of a technology of behavior must be submitted to the aims of a politics of freedom which constructs its concepts in a quite different universe of discourse.

On a third level *autonomous man* is a philosophical notion which deserves to be discussed according to its criteria of meaning which are neither those of a mentalistic psychology nor of a merely rhetorical politics, but those of a reflective and speculative philosophy. Professor Skinner may dislike philosophy, but he must agree that when Kant *created* "autonomy" as a philosophical concept he meant something which is completely overlooked in his book. I regret that under the title of the "literature of freedom and dignity" Professor Skinner systematically confuses bad psychology, anti-establishment pamphlets, and Kantian philosophy, to say nothing of those thinkers like Rousseau and Hegel who devoted whole books to the paradox of freedom and institutions, and who coined convenient philosophical concepts for that purpose which are badly lacking in Skinner's work.

I want now to consider these three points one after the other in hope of making sense of the concept of a technology of behavior without having to oppose it to a mixed and confused notion of "autonomous man."

MENTALISTIC PSYCHOLOGY

I want first to question the interpretation of "autonomous man" in terms of "mentalistic psychology." My claim is that the ethical and political implications concerning freedom, dignity, value, autonomy, etc., need not necessarily be conceived in terms of this psychology and that they are expressed better even in another language which has been explored during this last decade by phenomenologists and by the followers of Wittgenstein and Austin under the title of "linguistic analysis" of action, or "conceptual analysis in the theory of action." According to conceptual analysis, the network of concepts which we use to speak of *human action* in ordinary language is not the conceptual framework of either behaviorism or mentalistic psychology.

This first step is directly opposed to the claim of Professor Skinner's book that there is only one language-game with which we can speak significantly of human action. "Conceptual analysis" tends rather to show that human action is dependent on more than one language-game and that the behavioral sciences constitute only one of these games, ruled by specific demands which constitute "behavior" as something observable and homogeneous with other observables of the natural sciences such as physics and biology. The word "behavior" itself does not exhaust the meaning of the word "action." It merely indicates the previous choice of a certain language-game, with its semantics and its syntax, and it commits the user of this language-game to the rules which govern it. For example, it commits him not to speak of ideas, beliefs, of wanting (concepts which belong to another language-game) but rather to speak of "contingencies," "reinforcers," "control," "controller" and "controlled," etc. This language-game implies furthermore some rules for "translating"

49

what has already been said about action in other language-games into the idiom proper to the "behavior" language-game. Professor Skinner's book presents several examples of such translation. And the procedure is not objectionable as long as it is recognized for what it is. We may even assume that all that occurs in another language-game finds its translation into this language, even freedom, dignity and value. A language-game has its own coherence and it may claim to be complete within its own order.

But if some concepts are congenial to one language-game because they constitute it, others remain "translations." This is what happens in Professor Skinner's book. Undoubtedly "operant conditioning," "aversion reinforcers," even "intentional aversive control," "positive reinforcers," "contingencies of reinforcement," "countercontrol," and "escape from aversive control" constitute the "indigenous" vocabulary of behavior. But what about freedom, dignity, value? Is their "translation" equivalent to their original meaning? In other words, does their translation into the idiom of behavior occur without loss of meaning?

This question is legitimate insofar as it may be shown that the original idiom to which these expressions belong and from which they have been borrowed has more kinship with the language of ethics and politics than with the behavioristic language which leads to a technology, not to an ethics and a politics. But I will reserve this for the second part of my presentation. What I want to show now is that there are other ways of speaking of human action that are significant in the sense that statements produced in these other idioms are received and accepted by hearers in a way which allows them to respond verbally and practically in the endless process of interlocution and interaction.

"Mentalistic" language is a possible candidate for significant discourse about action. But it is not the only alternative language and may not be the most appropriate for discussing ethical and political issues. Nevertheless it has its own coherence. It is no less constructed than behavioristic language. It has been systematically constructed on the basis of a certain kind of philosophy which has its own criteria, which expresses these criteria and which establishes them as the axiomatics of the system. Hobbes, for example, decided to work only with entities which would be to the mind what "motion"—in the new Galilean sense of the word—is for bodies. Locke Descartes operate with "ideas" and reconstruct emotions, passions, feelings, etc., in terms of ideas with null-connotation. To these philosophical constructions we owe the wonderful "treatises on passions" of the seventeenth and eighteenth centuries and Hume's writings in moral philosophy. It may be said with confidence that these treatises have not been surpassed on their own ground. It is not without interest to recall that several of these writers also tried to derive a theory of freedom, dignity and value from their axiomatics of ideas, feelings, actions and passions. Hobbes remains the master in this endeavor, equalled only by Spinoza who derived all the major concepts of a political philosophy, such as power and sovereignty, from the theory of *conatus, actio, affectus, passio*, etc., established in

51

the *Ethics*. It would simply be ridiculous to object to Spinoza that the *conatus* is not an "observable" in the sense of the natural sciences. Such an objection begs the question since it starts from the presupposition that only "observables" are meaningful. The language of Spinoza has its own rules on intelligibility which are stated by the *Ethics* as a whole.

But I do not want to stay with the so-called "mentalistic" language, since my principal concern is to refute the series of dichotomies on which Professor Skinner's book relies. I want to consider the kind of philosophy of action, initiated by Wittgenstein and Austin, illustrated by such works as Anscombe's book on *Intention*, Melden's *Free Will*, C. R. Peter's *Motivation*, Richard Taylor's *Action and Purpose*, and Charles Taylor's *The Concept of Behavior*. This way of philosophizing about action consists in disentangling the conceptual framework underlying our use of expressions concerning action in ordinary language. The claim is that this use is meaningful, consistent, appropriate, unambiguous and received as such by human agents.

Three main implications result for our present discussion: first, the acknowledgment of the extraordinary diversity and complexity of this language which appears as the depository of a whole treasure of appropriate expressions progressively formed to cope with the infinite variety of human situations. This subtlety of ordinary language is well shown by the variety of questions which may be raised about a given action and which imply as many different and appropriate answers. Urmson, for example, lists no less than eight different questions which suggest a whole range of meanings for our concepts of motion and cause.

1. What was the point of his doing that?
2. What was his reason for doing that?
3. What led him to do that?
4. What prompted him to do that?
5. What made him do that?
6. What possessed him to do that?
7. How did he come to do that?
8. How did it come about that he did that?

"This list is certainly very incomplete (we can, for example, ask about a person's intentions or purpose) but it is long enough for the purpose which it has to serve. These questions are not perfectly precise, and admit, according to context, of being answered in more than one way; but there are fairly typical types of answers for some of them, and the answers appropriate to some of them would be quite inappropriate as answers to others."[1] According to some of these appropriate answers, a motive is a reason for and not a cause, for others a motive is also a cause, but not in the sense of a regular antecedent, but sometimes in the sense of a disposition, in other cases in the sense of an inner compulsion, or of an exterior constraint.

This analysis of the typical contexts in which appropriate answers are given to questions understood as meaningful by the hearers tends to show that there is more complexity in ordinary language than in the behavioristic language-game which claims to impose on us a simple choice between "autonomy" and "control exercised by the environment." Ordinary language displays a complicated and subtle range of intermediary cases which raise the most interesting questions concerning man.

A second benefit of this approach is to reveal not only the distinctiveness and the subtlety of ordinary language but its coherence. This language is not made of scattered expressions, but of expressions which define one another. If you have a language in which "purpose" is meaningful, you will find other expressions like "intention of . . . ," "intention with which," "reason for," "motive," "cause" (in one or the other senses of the word coherent with the system), and "agent." It is the whole network which makes sense. To understand one term is to have the mastery of the whole, in the same way as we acquire the competence of a linguistic system as a whole. What is fundamentally intelligible is "a person performs an action" or "a person can perform an action." All the terms are co-significant. To understand a statement of that form is to understand that a question such as "who did it?", "why?", "how?", etc., may receive an appropriate answer. It is not one of the least subtleties of this language-game that the same action requires a finite answer to the question "who?" and an infinite inquiry into motives and causes in answer to the question "why?" To identify someone and to explain in terms of motives and causes are two complementary operations.

This second group of remarks tends to say that there are several "grammars" of action and that the so-called "scientific" one does not have the monopoly of meaningfulness and coherence.

A third advantage of an approach through ordinary language is to repudiate from the start *dualistic* notions. Human action takes place endlessly on the borderline between the "interior" and the "exterior." Or rather, it denies all language which proceeds from their opposition. Such false problems as the causation of "movements" by "ideas," or in general the action of the "soul" on the "body" proceed from a *wrong grammar* of the language-game of action. This is the main argument of the theory of action against "mentalistic" theories. As I said, those theories have their own intelligibility and coherence. But they fail precisely on this problem of the transition from "idea" to "movement." The behaviorist may welcome this critique as parallel to his own. But the theorist of action will object to the behaviorist that he takes only the second half of the broken unity. His notion of contingency or of reinforcement presupposes the same breakdown of the indivisible unity of man as does the mentalistic psychology. Both psychologies are by-products of the same metaphysics which produced on the one hand the "idea" and on the other hand "movement." All the fundamental concepts of action are *mixed* concepts. The expression "I can" conveys their kernel-experience. It implies a relation between the ego and his own body which links interiority and exteriority. On the one hand, I may express my action in terms of intentions or reasons and invoke excuses; on the other hand, I may express my action in terms of the things which it changes; but the most interesting expressions—like "showing" and "grasping"—imply the kind of indivisible existence which precedes the distinction between interior and exterior.

At that stage an ontology of the *corps propre* in the sense of Merleau-Ponty and existential phenomenology seems to be inescapable as the *pre-understanding* on which the functioning of our language in ordinary life relies.

This kind of reflection concerning the conditions of possibility of a discourse about human action is completely overlooked by Professor Skinner's book. This is why he so easily takes for granted the dichotomy of "inner" man and "environmental" contingencies. My claim is that the kind of conflict on which this book relies already expresses the loss of the ordinary ground on which a discourse on action can be displayed in a meaningful way.

WILD FREEDOM

In the second part of my discussion, I should like to consider the objection raised to the "literature of freedom and dignity" by Professor Skinner. What is at stake here is the claim of "wild" freedom, the chaotic advocacy of spontaneity.

For clarity of discussion we must distinguish between this new set of notions and the "mentalistic" theory which we mentioned earlier. If it is true that the claim for uncontrolled freedom has some kinship with the theory of "inner man" and "mental states," it adds something of a different order, i.e., the affirmation that all regulation is bad. Professor

B. F. *Skinner's* Beyond Freedom and Dignity

Skinner translates: "All control is wrong." (41) And he has no difficulty in showing that human behavior is controlled and reinforced by external contingencies. He concludes that the problem is to change contingencies, not states of mind.

But this second alternative seems to me as questionable as the first one. I do not feel obliged to choose between wild freedom or a technology of behavior. Or, if you prefer, I have as much sympathy for the one as for the other: for the technology of behavior and its appropriate criticism of the illusion of immediate freedom; or for the claim of freedom and its affirmation that freedom is something other than contingency.

My problem deals with a question that is prior to this sterile dichotomy. This is the question of the relation between freedom and institutions. But the elaboration of this question requires a specific conceptual apparatus in which these words receive their proper meaning. This conceptual apparatus implies, it seems to me, ordinary language about action, but adds to it a new dimension which belongs to neither behavioristic nor mentalistic language— not even to ordinary language.

That ordinary language about action is presupposed seems obvious. The problem of freedom and institutions, on which I want to focus now, presupposes that man may *designate* his actions as his intentions, *justify* them by the reasons for which he claims to perform them, and *ascribe* them to himself as the agent of his own doing. If this language is meaningless, or if it means nothing objective, it would be useless to ask further whether an intention is right, a reason legitimate, or an agent responsible. Of course it is feasible to "translate" this language into the idiom of behavior in order to develop a science of observation applied to man; but it will be necessary to return from this translation to the original text to raise the central problem designated by the title *Beyond Freedom and Dignity.* In other words, it is within the language game of "action as performed by a person" that ethical and political problems make sense.

But, on the other hand, a fruitful discussion concerning freedom and institutions requires a new set of concepts which are not included in a so-called theory of action. What we want here is not only a sense for the *plurality* of the universes of discourse in which we may speak of human action, but a sense for the *hierarchy* of problems implied here. While concepts like intention, purpose, motive, agent, etc. may be enough to define "a person performs an action," they no longer suffice to give an account of ethical and political issues.

The key concept of this new conceptual framework, it seems to me, is that of *institution.* It covers all kinds of social bodies in which the individual plays a role in accordance with *rules* which prescribe a behavior which contributes to the functioning of the whole body. It is mainly because man belongs to institutions—professional, social, political, religious institutions—that he appears as a rule-following animal. Now, is the rule-following purpose pattern into which we fit our common sense description of "man within institutions" only a particular case of what Professor Skinner calls "contingencies"? Even if we add the adjective, "social"? Economists and political scientists require more specific concepts related to the kind of "rules" which define the different social games in which man is involved. And each sphere of activity develops its own conceptual framework which requires a different conceptual analysis. A general theory of institutions requires a subtle dialectic of spheres and levels in which the concepts belonging to one sphere or level are suppressed and retained in the following one. From this point of view, the concept of a technology of behavior is too little dialectical, too univocal. It would be more effective if it did not claim to cover the whole field of freedom and institutions, and deliberately limited itself to the contribution of the psychologist to a *politics of freedom.* This contribution is surely more important than the man in the street or the professional politician may think, and even more important than the economist or the political scientist would be ready to acknowledge. In that sense, this book is a claim for recognition of the part of the psychologist in the great endeavor of planning human life. But inasmuch as the psychologist is unable to *locate* his contribution in the symphony of sciences and therefore to *limit* his claim, his concept of a technology of behavior must appear as ill-founded. A technology has the same extension as the corresponding science. A technology of behavior has the same scope as a science of behavior, i.e., as psychology. Economics and political science rely on other sets of concepts and develop other kinds of technologies. We cannot put all "the conditions of which behavior is a function" (12) under one and the same discipline. The same may be said of all the so-called "social environments" (15) and all the ways in which "control [is] exercised by the environment." (21) "Environment" and "control" are too loose as concepts to cover all the hierarchies of institutional patterns implied in the different social spheres of activity. Therefore a technology of behavior is a valid concept only as long as it remains a careful extrapolation from the study of "operant" behavior which the psychologist may observe "by arranging environments in which specific consequences are contingent upon it." (18) I speak of a careful extrapolation because the concept of technology remains limited by the manipulation of the environment. This concept is not commensurate with the whole pattern of a politics of freedom. At most, it is a part of a politics of freedom. It cannot be the whole.

Now, who sees the whole? Maybe nobody. At least, nobody as a scientist approaching man from this or that point of view, i.e., from the point of view of the kind of "rules" defining a specific social framework. It is the task of another kind of reflection, of a *philosophical anthropology*, to delineate the sphere of validity, to reconnect what the scientific procedures necessarily isolate, to try to understand the whole dialectic at stake between the different institutional spheres, and to reopen the game which the partial fanaticisms tend to close according to the imperialistic concepts of one discipline.

In that sense the philosophical task is not to deny the concept and the project of a technology of behavior, but to locate it correctly within a larger framework.

B. F. *Skinner's* Beyond Freedom and Dignity

This methodological and epistemological discussion has already led us to the *speculative* implications of the problem of *autonomy*. As I said in my introductory remarks, autonomy is not a word from popular philosophy or pamphlet-literature, but of technical and sophisticated philosophizing. It belongs by priority to the Kantian vocabulary. Even if I am more inclined to discuss the issues at stake in Professor Skinner's book within an Hegelian framework of thought, I cannot forget that Hegel received the problem of "freedom made actual" from Kant who had *thought* the concept of autonomy and led it to its most radical conditions of possibility. Essentially these conditions are not denied but incorporated into the Hegelian endeavor. They deserve to be recalled in order to clarify the concept of "autonomous man" against which Professor Skinner argues.

It must first be well understood that this concept is a *practical* concept, not in the sense of *behavioral*, but in the sense that its assertion derives from no descriptive statement. We do not *state* freedom. Therefore we can neither prove it nor deny it on factual grounds. It is not an "observable," either to inner or external perception. It is neither seen nor felt. It is not a "theoretical" concept. This is why it belongs neither to the language-game of "behavior," nor to that of "mental states," not even to that of "human action" (in the ordinary language use). All these language-games can be shown to depend on the *Critique of Pure Reason*, i.e., of theoretical reason. Autonomy is not something which exists, it is a task to be achieved. It *is* not, it *has to be.* The concept of "man," in the last chapter of Professor Skinner's book relies finally on a "practical" assertion of this kind and belongs to those sets of concepts of which Kant said they "extend" our reason without increasing our knowledge.

Secondly, we owe to Kant the demonstration that freedom is a practical concept because the kind of law to which it is linked is not a law in the sense of the laws of nature, but a non-empirical law, an obligation. In other words, we must think freedom and norms together. Law is the *ratio intelligendi* of freedom; freedom is the *ratio essendi* of law.

We are here at the core of the problem raised by *Beyond Freedom and Dignity.* The link which correlates freedom and law denies as much the dream of a freedom without laws as the idea of a law which would not be from the beginning a law of freedom. This is why the popular literature about wild freedom is empty, just as the concept of a technology of behavior is ill-founded.

What we must think about is a rule-governed freedom. And that is precisely *auto-nomy.*

A third debt to Kant must be recalled: there is no ethical, no political problem, if we do not take into account from the very start a principle of *mutuality* from person to person. I dare say that the problem of freedom, and maybe, before all, that of dignity, is raised in the first place with the second person: *your* freedom, *your* dignity, comes first. The recognition of another freedom, the position of the *other* as having as much value as I have, are primitive acts which can be derived from nothing else. Why *should* we not kill, if it were useful, reinforcing? Here is the fundamental limit of any technology of behavior, since it cannot take into account the notion of a person as "an end in itself" which is constitutive of the concept of dignity. To have a value and not a price, that is to have dignity, according to Kant. But the position of the ethical problem on the basis of the second person is no less a denial of the illusion of lawless freedom. Ethical freedom is not a claim which proceeds from me and is opposed to any control; it is, rather, a demand which is addressed to me and which proceeds from the other: allow me to exist in front of you, as your equal! Dignity is the demand of freedom at the second person level. There would be no question of treating the person in myself as an end in itself, if I did not meet this requirement with reference to the other. In that sense, I am my own neighbor, because I am the neighbor of my neighbors. Therefore freedom is no longer an extension of my attempt to escape control or to avoid constraint. It is an extension of my recognition of the equal right of the other to exist.

But this notion of the person—of the second person, if the expression is not tautological—remains a practical and normative concept. The person cannot be observed from without; nor felt from within. We "treat" somebody as a person; the person is a way of acting, not of knowing. That the person 'exists as an end, nobody can state it; we *have to* make it true.

This way of introducing freedom on the basis of dignity, and dignity on the basis of the practical concept of the person, allows us to relate directly the concept of *value*, studied by Professor Skinner in his sixth chapter, to the ethical sphere of concepts. Here too, we must refuse a deceptive dichotomy: *either* the concept of value remains purely metaphysical, as a Platonic idea, or it has to be derived from the behavioral concept of "reinforcer." The idea of value, it seems to me, is the condition of possibility for the co-existence of several persons, for the mutuality of free beings. "Justice" is not a celestial entity, it is the rule for arbitrating opposing claims. It is therefore dependent on the idea that *your* freedom precedes mine. The first "value" is that the other exists as a person. In that sense, nothing is more concrete: it is the "face" of the other, as Emmanuel Lévinas says, that tells me, in negative terms: "Don't kill me!"—and in more positive terms: "Love me! I am another you."

I do not want to say that this concept of *autonomy* is enough to found ethics and politics. In that sense, Professor Skinner is right. Something is lacking concerning the *actualization* of freedom, something which is the topic of the Hegelian philosophy. But the foundations are laid. And they are not denied by what has to be added. All that I said in the second part of my remarks presupposes the kind of radical justification which I just outlined. The problem of freedom and of institutions has to be built on the basis of practical, normative and intersubjective concepts, such as those which Kant established. There would be no problem of "making freedom *actual*," if freedom was not posited in that practical, normative and intersubjective way. A technology of behavior, fully justified at its own level, belongs to this endeavor to pass from a *critique* of ethical concepts to an *actualization* of freedom.

But we must be aware of the requirements of such an endeavor to embrace not only the conditions of possibility of freedom in a Kantian sense, but the conditions of its actualization in a Hegelian sense.

The first requirement is a logical one. We are unable to handle the huge problems raised by the interconnections between the different spheres of actualization of freedom without a *dialectical* logic. By this I mean a way of thinking which gives an account of the conceptual discontinuities between the spheres and nevertheless preserves the continuity of sedimentation from level to level. Such is the kind of logic which rules Hegel's *Philosophy of Right*, which could also be called, *Beyond Freedom and Dignity*. Beyond mere *Sollen*, towards *Wirklichkeit*. Beyond the foundation, toward the actualization. According to this ambitious program, Hegel proceeds from abstract right to subjective morality, from morality to objective ethics, and within this concrete ethics, from the structure of family life to the systems of economic life and then to the constitution of the State. Thus the conceptual novelty of each sphere of problems and the cumulative achievement of the whole process are preserved at the same time.

I do not intend that we should have to repeat Hegel and rewrite his *Philosophy of Right*. I only claim that our present task is similar to that of Hegel: to elaborate the theoretical framework within which the partial results of the several human sciences could make sense—including the science of behavior and the technology of behavior. This task remains a *dialectical* task, since the results of one stage can be preserved in the following one only under the conditions of the conceptual novelty of this stage.

It is too obvious that this dialectical sense is alien to Professor Skinner's work. Hence the kind of *monotony* of his conceptual apparatus and the hazardous extrapolation of one set of concepts beyond their initial sphere of validity.

If we concede the dialectical character of the problems implied here, the initial dichotomy on which Professor Skinner's book relies loses its strength. "Environment" and "autonomous man" are mere abstractions with reference to the whole process of freedom made actual. What we want is a basic way of thinking in which the opposition between "inner man" and "external contingencies" is overcome and radically defined. The concepts of "institutions of freedom" and "actualization of freedom" present from the very start this dialectical constitution. This is why they put us beyond the opposite claims of a freedom without laws and a scientific analysis which "shifts both the responsibility and the achievements to the environment." (25) Dialectical concepts impose the necessity to think together the progression of "inner man" and the construction of the historical patterns which give sense to human action. "Autonomous man" and "external contingencies" are dialectically linked.

Because this dialectical constitution of the concepts of "freedom and dignity" is not recognized, Professor Skinner's book has to work with concepts which are the non-dialectical counterparts of equally non-dialectical concepts. His plea for "exteriority" remains

66

the reverse side of his opponents' concept of "interiority." For the same reason, his technology remains a technology of "exteriority," which has the same limitations as the anti-technology preached by the advocates of "felt" freedom.

In other words, what is required is a mode of thought which would not oppose but correlate "the autonomous man of traditional theory" and "the achievements of the environment."

NOTES

1. J. O. Urmson, "Motives and Causes" in *The Philosophy of Action*, ed. Alan R. White (Oxford: Oxford University Press, 1968), p. 153.

3

What Does Humanism Mean?

WHAT DOES HUMANISM MEAN FOR US IN THE MIDDLE of this century? It seems to me that it is impossible to extract the essential points of a "politics of culture" without doing the preliminary work of sorting out meanings. This effort of discriminating true and living meanings which perhaps conceal superficial significations and dead pretensions appears already as our most significant task, which is to project our role—if one understands by "role" both the revindication of the place for and the recognition of a service connected with the man of culture.

In the minor sense of the word, the question of "humanism" coincides with that of the "humanities" and, even more narrowly, with the ancient heritage of European culture. It helps to situate the problem within the most modest limits, such as those posed, for example, by the framework of the school and the university, before taking the larger step to the

Translated by David Stewart

cultural life of a people. (Additionally this cultural life, which to a great extent is co-extensive with the life of leisure, is itself nourished, in the final analysis, by a scholarly heritage). Reflection on the ancient heritage at the level of studies leads in fact to the essentials of the problems which over-lap the notion of humanism. If our attachment to the ancient heritage of our culture is to be anything other than a simple prejudice, it is necessary that we find again the very meaning of our whole "heritage," which is the function of every cultural "memory," in a humanism and an élan of humanity more profound than simple respect for the past.

The safeguarding of the ancient heritage, to which we provisionally are reducing the problem of humanism, calls for two groups of reflections which correspond to two groups of disputes to which this ancient heritage is subject.

The ancient heritage is first placed in question by another type of culture which also claims the title "humanities" and which is often designated by the elegant name of "modern humanities." This dispute is tied to a more general fact: in spite of the eighteenth century, we have moved beyond a cultural system which was almost exclusively determined by our Mediterranean past to a cultural system more widely determined by the living cultures of the entire world. The Greco-Latin culture *behind* us and the foreign culture *beside* us challenge each other and our-selves for supremacy, and our ancient memory is more and more inhibited by the vagueness of present cultures, as if the world-wide present were submerging the Mediterranean past at the very heart of our understanding and sensibility. The debate between two types of "humanities," the one the basis of dead languages, the other the basis of living languages, is therefore the reflection of a more profound debate which underlies our culture. The less we are bound to our Greco-Latin past the more we are bound to the living cultures of the present world.

Humanism in the narrow sense presents itself as a resistance to this tendency of modern man to disengage himself from his cultural past; in short, humanism is a resistance to forgetfulness. What justifies this resistance if, once again, it is to be more than an irrational piety exhibited by certain learned persons imprisoned in a bookish culture? It is justified by the function of memory itself in the heart of a culture. A cultural being is not a *mens instantanea*; it is not necessary to surrender oneself to the tide of contradictory influences of the modern world without re-rooting oneself in their origins. It is not possible to conserve an original cultural personality without a living tradition. The Greco-Latin culture is the privileged means by which a soul struggling increasingly against cultural exoticism regains its equilibrium. It is necessary to have a memory in order to have a self, and a self encounters others in order to receive something from them without being destroyed by the communication.

But memory, in turn, is not a simple phenomenon of passive preservation; antiquity survives in us through successive *renewals* of antiquity, through the series of renaissances—the Carolingian Renaissance, the Renaissance of the seventeenth century, and the "Renaissance," properly called, of European and French classicism. The men of the French Revolution were still Romans nourished by Tacitus and Plutarch.

This is why the defense of the ancient humanities loses all meaning if it is reduced to a sterile repetition of literary products and pure esthetic forms, especially if one loses the testimony of humanity that these works transmit to us. To imitate the ancients is to do as they did, that is, to create a civilization.

It is true that this problem of cultural memory has taken on a new form in our day. The unmeasured richness and complexity of modern civilization prohibits a single person today from encompassing the ancient past, foreign cultures, and sciences and technology in a personal culture. We now need a "polyphonic conception of culture where the parts, interacting but distinct, will be assumed by the one or the other, *diversis diversa.*"[1] Also, "humanists" today can no longer pretend to be microcosms of culture; they are irremediably men of the past and experts of cultural memory. But that is not without its dangers, for the *anachronistic* function of today's humanism is incontestably more fragile than the totalizing function of the humanism of the Renaissance. Still, it is not necessary to exaggerate the total and integral character of certain of the great minds of the Renaissance, even less their role of gathering together the culture of their time. These sovereign and synoptic minds were themselves mingled with a powerfully contradictory history. Some even presided over gigantic cultural disintegrations (science and theology, ethics and politics, Reformation and Renaissance, universality and nationality, etc.). This is why the humanism of modern man is not appreciably different from successive humanisms, all of which were "renewals" and even veritable recreations of the ancient heritage and all of which were prey to the contradiction of modernity and reminiscence.

We have defined humanism by the "humanities" and the latter by the ancient heritage faced with the pressure of modern cultures. A second, larger circle is drawn around this narrow meaning of the term, and at the same time a more profound intention raises itself with this new meaning. This second circle is that of *culture as leisure*.

We will discover this new dimension of the problem under the cover of a reflection on the place of work and the technical activities of man. A new tension appears here, one that is not so much between the two poles of our "humanities" (classical and modern) as between these humanities (considered less as a scholarly theme for study than as sustenance of a life of leisure and of a disinterested cultural activity), and the activity of man which is utilitarian, laborious, and professional. Here again we have to recover for this conflict the balanced tensions of our modernity.

We are by no means condemned to protest foolishly against the "invasion of technology," the "leveling of culture," or the "disappearance of the elites." The humanist willingly takes the posture of the man besieged by the rising tide who flees to the heights but who flees without hope, knowing that the high rock of his refuge will finally be submerged. We would be very wrong to think that disinterested culture, of which Greek science is the archetype, is condemned in the end to revel in a bitter consciousness of a postponed death.

The evolution of technology itself makes an appeal to this humanism based on a disinterested culture. Technologists themselves tell us that the delay in specialization is a factor of adjustment in the modern world. An adjustment of high quality requires a kind of professional mobility, flexibility, and co-ordination between special techniques. In short, a superior adaptation must be culturally dominated. Culture thus appears as a "great detour" between man and his powers.

But all this is still not the most important aspect of the problem. Leisure, disengaged by productivity from work, now poses a problem as important as that of adjustment to work. Nevertheless, every culture must be prepared for work *and* for leisure, for the rhythm of work-leisure. But the man of leisure, a user and no longer a producer, does not have to solve a technical problem of adaptation but an ethical problem of mastery. But how are we to exercise this mastery over the objects of our enjoyment without a certain disdain for these objects? It is here that the function of culture appears and with it a second sense of humanism that we are seeking to delineate. Every culture tends not only to slow down the adaptation of the working man but to detach the man of leisure from the goods that a consumer economy places before him to meet his needs. Culture is this carry-over from the desirability of immediate goods produced by a technological civilization towards goods more difficult to approach, that is, toward more unusual and complex pleasures. This function of the lack of adaptation with respect to objects of elementary desirability introduces us to the very heart of humanism beyond the purely "literary" concern of safeguarding a received heritage.

Humanism, then, appears as the reply to the peril of the "objectification" of man in work and in consuming. The technological condition of modern work and the bewitchment of techniques of consuming and well-being give rise to a menace which does not seem to be able to lead beyond the "alienations" that Marx tied to the exploitation of work by the capitalist vampire. Perhaps the modern evolution of work only makes evident a profound tendency of work to absorb us in the end by selling us out. This tendency appears to me irreducible to "alienation," which in the proper sense of the word is the loss of self not only in another but for the profit of another who exploits the intention of man and robs him of his humanity. Alienation poses a social and, finally, a political problem; objectification, a cultural problem. The curious thing is that well-being evokes the same objectification as work, especially in its fragmented form.

The function, then, not only of the "humanities" but of every disinterested, cultural activity—and especially philosophy—is its struggle against "objectification," through reflection and meditation. It compensates for the adaptation of the workingman to a finite work, as well as for the man of well-being with a restricted pleasure, through the consideration of the Open, as Rilke said. Humanism is this very

74

movement of compensation by culture for objectification.

These reflections on culture understood as "leisure" have indeed already drawn us beyond our point of departure. Humanism, we said at first, is the "humanities" and, more precisely, the classical humanities—that is, in the final analysis and through a series of historical "renewals," the *ancient heritage.* The great rhythm of work and leisure has constrained us to enlarge considerably the horizon of the problem and to identify humanism with the *collection of disinterested* cultural activities which compensate man in his work and well-being.

It is necessary to say more. Up to this point we have only looked for the meaning of humanism in activities of defense and compensation: defense against the pressure of non-classical, "modern" humanities, and compensation for technology. It is as though humanism were reduced to the "counterpole" of modernity. More profoundly, it is necessary to look at the very heart of the civilizing movement: humanism is not only the "humanities," in the literary and artistic sense, but the "élan of humanity" in the ethico-cultural sense.

I would say, at this third level of our investigation, that humanism is this preliminary conviction that through the material determinations of a civilization —geographic, technological, and economic determinations—man determines and chooses himself, and that this choice can be clarified and reflected on and thus improved by the activity of men of culture. Humanism is therefore this preliminary conviction that the activity of men of culture is efficacious with an efficaciousness exactly proportioned to its disinterestedness—not in spite of its disinterestedness but to the extent of its disinterestedness.

What does this conviction signify? And why just call it "preliminary"? I have called it preliminary because it cannot be claimed by any *science* of civilization. It is of the order of a wager; or better, it is a sort of initial investment made by the cultural function in the dynamics of societies. It is an investment which is not theoretically but practically justified, that is, by the very devotion that this investment engenders and which in turn raises it. Even as "metaphysical" freedom is not of the order of proof but of an awakening, the call of the self, so it can only be believed actively or acted on thoughtfully— in the same way the role of the man of culture cannot be determined empirically but can only be presupposed with conviction as a *rational belief* in the possibility of existing historically as a man of culture. In the Kantian sense of the word, it is a "postulate" of practical reason; that is, act according to the reasonable maxim of the man of culture and you will believe that the existential possibility of your activity is tied to a certain structure of history just as your existence has a *power* over this history. Not only will you believe it, but you will verify it, for the belief of the man of culture in his own efficaciousness belongs to the very conditions of this efficaciousness. But you will never know for sure; you will neither know from science *whether* the life of culture is efficacious nor *how* it is efficacious. In order to know that, there would have to exist an empirical science of the *total* composition of causalities in

76

the dynamics of societies, with the maxim of the man of culture belonging to this total composition. That is impossible, for the life of culture would then no longer be itself but a "natural" force, and freedom itself would be the object of sight and no longer an act. The absence of such a science bearing on the total meaning of the dynamics of societies is therefore not tied to a provisional infirmity of the human sciences; it is a consequence of the hyperempirical character of the maxim of freedom enveloped by the cultural act. This is why the conviction of the efficaciousness of the life of culture must remain a risk and a gamble both in the reading of events and in the project of the tasks to be undertaken. It is more "practice" than "theory," as an Awakening, a Renaissance, a Reformation.

Nevertheless, this conviction is not at all blind and irrational. Humanism, as belief in the historical efficaciousness of the life of culture, is not a groundless fideism. Risky as act, this belief is rational in its *restraint*. In effect, what does it emphasize? It affirms that in every civilization one can recover those values in motion which give this civilization an option or a consent to these values. These values, of course, are more experienced and acted on than reflected on. They are "crystallized" in the fashions of life, customs, and political conduct. As such, they are the *open direction* of this civilization. It is to this operated and operating meaning that the cultural act is added and applied. The man of culture recaptures these values "crystallized" in the mish-mash of collective conduct. It is this "renewal" which gives a reasonable content to the belief in the proper efficaciousness of the cultural act in which we have recognized the meaning of humanism. If, for example, the Renaissance was able to revitalize the ancient heritage, it was by a renewal of certain values embodied in the works and the conduct of Greek and Roman man.

The link between the first definitions that we have given of humanism and that which we now propose is this: a "heritage" only survives through a "renewal." Humanism, as the maintenance of the ancient heritage, is only the *inverse* of humanism as a present cultural invention. Humanism in the first sense is therefore only the shadow of humanism in the sense that we are now speaking of.

And in what does this "renewal" consist? I see in it a "critical" aspect and a "poetic" aspect.

On the one hand, humanism is always a "critique" in the sense that the "élan of humanity" (to pick up again the vague expression invoked earlier) proceeds reflexively through a discernment and an evaluation of civilizing types, manners of being, and styles of life implicit in an epoch. One easily recovers this critical function in the novel, the theater, the essay, in philosophy, in painting (as one ponders the work of Picasso's *Guernica*), and gradually in all the arts. This "critical" function therefore extends philosophic activity, in the narrow sense of the word, although one should say that it is the implicit philosophy of the cultural act in general.

Whether it be a critique of the philistine, the bourgeois, or the fascist, a critique of the militant or the esthete, of the racist or of the utopian, a critique of the world of money or a critique of

78

technology, the humanistic thrust of a work consists in this task of elucidation, of denunciation, of correction, and of advancement which presupposes its own efficaciousness—that is, the leverage on history of consciousness, of lucidity, and of reflection. Such being its orientation, the "critic" believes in his efficaciousness precisely as critic; and this belief is humanism itself—or at least the better half of its negative function. This critical activity, applied directly or indirectly to a particular "figure" or to a particular "limited-profile" in order to discern in it a "non"-civilization or a "pseudo"-civilization, makes the man of culture the man of protest and denunciation.

In turn, this "critical" function is only the inverse of a "poetic" function. Because the man of culture is not concerned with *political* efficaciousness proper (which is the measure of all projects by means of the capture of power or the exercise of power), he has at his disposal in the long run an efficaciousness on the deeper level of representations and guiding images which orient a civilization toward well-being or toward force, toward stagnation or expansion, toward a particular conception of education, or toward a particular "system" of relations between the economic, the social, the political, and the cultural. To the very extent that the man of culture is not concerned with the political realization of his ideas, he *opens up the horizon of possibilities.* In this way he co-operates in the promotion of a new man without knowing absolutely what sort of man is arising or how he arises. It is thus that humanism is "revolutionary" par excellence; it draws man ahead by projecting his meaning. Whether he dreams, paints, or creates fictional persons, the man of culture is present at the heart of reality, particularly if he has not intended to be.

We have gone as far is possible with an interpretation of humanism as resistance to modernity with the help of classical "humanities." Far from being a closed garden in which the learned person is shielded from civilization, humanism appears on the contrary as the affirmative power of civilization itself, through the critical and creative activity of men of culture.

We will draw certain consequences from this belief in the efficaciousness of the "critical" and "poetic" function of culture in the threefold direction of ethics, politics, and a philosophy of culture.

First, it seems to me that the man of culture must not at all be ashamed of being an "intellectual."

True, this feeling sometimes haunts him. The status of the "intellectual" in past societies was so much responsible for the ancient opposition between the "liberal" and the "servile" that the ascent of a civilization of work through communism, as well as through the socialist transformations of liberal democracies, appears to place in question the very status of the intellectual.

Reflection on the critical and poetic function of the man of culture is what gives both a meaning and a limit to this self-doubt. Even if the opposition between the free man and the slave had been the sociological form in which the function of the intellectual was constituted and developed, this sociological form never exhausted its radical intention. A single slave philosophy in antiquity attests that the cultural function had never been defined entirely by the social situation of the man of leisure faced with the slave. It is this radical intention that one must continuously recover in order to project its incarnation in the order of a civilization of work—that is, of a civilization where work would be the dominant economic and social category.

It seems to me that this radical intention is the inalienable function of *Speech*. The dignity of speech is by no means diminished by the recovered or even discovered dignity of work. A fundamental dialectic of human existence in all its intensity arises, instead, in the very context of the promotion of the workingman in the dialectic of speech and work. Because we know better than any other epoch that man is fundamentally a worker, we can likewise understand better than any epoch that the function of speech is irreducible. To want to say, to signify, finally to say, is by no means to produce something by muscle power or by means of a tool or a machine. It is to give the lumination of meaning to the force of what is to be done. It is this lumination that is efficacious. Words that have renounced the world in order to transform it are what have had the most intense mediating efficaciousness—such as those of Parmenides and those of Euclid.

Certainly the economic-social degradation of work by capitalist exploitation has had as its counterpart a dignity usurped by speech—the speech of the negotiator, the businessman, the lawyer, the professor, the writer. Speech has become an added means of exploiting work. In this sense there is a culpability of culture to the extent that it has served the degradation of work.

But if speech is guilty of the exploitation of work, it is originally innocent in the sense that it is "the clarifying light of every man coming in this world." That is why I am able to regret the *misuse* of speech but never its *goal*. Guarded by this *goal* of speech, the man of culture is vindicated.

Our reflections on the critical and poetic role of the man of culture leads to the definition that I will call the true liberalism as a fundamental principle of a politics of culture.

Because we never know—with absolute knowledge —in what sense and by what means the man of culture co-operates in the movement of civilization, a politics of culture necessarily includes *on the part of political man this faith*, which is both a wager and a hazard. The wager is that useless man, loquacious man, protesting man, the dreamer and utopian, is the bearer of an undeniable efficaciousness. The risk is that the man of culture, who appears to be contributing something because he says expected things, is finally an artisan of stagnation and perhaps of dissolution, whereas the negative individual appears in reality to be the herald of a new epoch. Although the State has always hesitated to pursue this wager and risk, it is the modern political consciousness that has most repudiated it. Here also, as is usually the case regarding the civilization of work, the resistances to a liberal politics of culture are not derived from reason. The political consciousness, in the strong sense of the word, does not have two periods. I understand by political consciousness the recognition of the fact that life in the State is not a sector of existence among others but an agreement among all the interests and all the tasks of human existence. In short, the State is an embracing totality with relation to economic and social life and also with relation to customs, the sciences, and to the arts. Culture is therefore embraced in a certain manner in politics. That is true even of the most liberal State. To the extent that it is a State, it has a politics of culture with a certain direction. One need not refer to wartime, revolution, or a grave crisis in order to see censorship extending its hideous inquisition over every work of the spirit. Censorship is an extreme form and caricature of the essence of the State as a hypercultural reality. And it is because modern man has more exactly recognized the hegemonious function of the State and the complexity of the rationality of the reality which constitutes it that there is now an acute problem of the politics of culture.

What does humanism mean when facing this situation? It means the revindication of true liberalism, that is, the revindication of an arena recognized and guaranteed by the State for critical and creative activity of the man of culture. This revindication is the corollary of the belief with which we have identified humanism—the belief in the efficaciousness of cultural activity *in the absence of any absolute knowledge* relating to the ways and means of this efficaciousness.

Humanism is therefore politically the refusal of a purely apologetic conception of culture. It is anticlerical in the precise sense of the word; in the same way as it formerly refused to bend the truth of the investigations of the sciences and the arts before ecclesiastical authority, it refuses in our day to bend before political authority.

This refusal is wise, for state management of culture, as ecclesiastical management, is finally a bad calculation. An artist who choses to be useful or edifying will immediately cease to be a creator. Artists, writers, and thinkers serve society best when they serve without knowing or intending to, that is, by remaining faithful to the internal problems of their art and their meditation, and with the most demanding impulse issuing from themselves. The so-called "engaged" literature risks repeating purely and simply what the consciousness of an epoch has already ceased to create, only to be seduced by the very banality of its vision of the world. On the contrary, that literature accused of being "disengaged" risks, under the cover of its very retreat, elaborating a new expectation which anticipates the man of tomorrow.

The State therefore ought not to rush in and prescribe a near and visible efficaciousness to the man of culture. If the credo of humanism is the efficaciousness of the man of culture *as such*, this credo has as its political corollary that this efficaciousness is neither measurable by the man of culture nor by the State. Precisely because this efficaciousness can never be known but only believed and willed, it remains a sort of risk for the writer and the artist, *but also for the State*. To be sure, this revindication of true liberalism evokes more problems than it resolves. We well know that the rising needs of the modern world call for an extensive plan of economic life and therefore a national direction for the collection of productive activities of the nations. It is not easy to find an agreement between this demand and that of a liberal politics of culture. This is perhaps the greatest problem of our time. Perhaps one should even admit that we are only on the threshold of the problem. The pressure of needs on technology is such that all economic plans have something of the premature and the barbarous. In this state of the infancy of the problem of the *connection between economic planning and cultural liberalism*, it is doubtless inevitable that the "critical" function of culture and its "poetic" function will pose the specter of an anarchist revindication in regard to political consciousness. But this anarchist appearance of the humanist revindication is the other side of the barbarous appearance of economic planning. Together, these two appearances constitute what I would call the infancy of the problem.

The right to self-esteem which is appropriate for the man of culture, the liberal revindication which appears to implicate him in the face of political power, leads finally to a *philosophy* implicit in every humanism. Humanism, we have said, professes the efficaciousness of the man of culture but without his "knowing" it. It is this non-knowledge that we must now decide upon.

I see humanism, in the last instance, as a *philosophy* of limits. We do not know everything; we do not even know how work and speech, politics and culture, economic planning and free esthetic creation are articulated. From time to time we detect the limited dialectics that we have already tried to extrapolate, but the total meaning escapes us.

This philosophy of limits belongs both to a Christian and Kantian strain of thought. When Christian thought speaks of a Last Day, the function of this "mythical" theme—in the strong sense of the word—is always to shatter the pretensions of absolute knowledge played by the role of the Last Judgment in regard to the totality of history. Eschatology keeps history open by adding the final meaning. It joins, in this function, the limit-idea in the Kantian sense. I think everything and I demand everything, but I am never able to know it. Kant only applied to cosmology his golden rule of the limiting function of the concept of the thing-in-itself. But it is necessary to apply to the totality of history this *limiting* role of the idea of its total meaning and to raise it up against all pretensions that would say what this total meaning is. That is the fundamental principle of the thesis according to which the efficaciousness of the man of culture, and its corollary in a liberal politics of culture, is the object of belief and not of knowledge.

Why still call this philosophy of limits a humanism? Because the word *human* in humanism sums up all its meaning. Man is man when he knows that he is *only* man. The ancients called man a "mortal." This "remembrance of death" indicated in the very *name* of man introduces the reference to a limit at the very heart of the affirmation of man himself. When faced with the pretension of absolute knowledge, humanism is therefore the indication of an "only": we are *only* men.

What Does Humanism Mean?

No longer "human, all too human": this formula still shares in the intoxication of absolute knowledge; but "only human." This formula protects the sobriety of humanism.

NOTES

1. Henri-Irenee Marrou, "L'Avenir de la culture classique," *Esprit* 23 (February, 1955), p. 184.

4

VIOLENCE AND LANGUAGE

THE IMPORTANCE OF THIS SUBJECT DERIVES FROM THE fact that the confrontation of violence with language underlies all of the problems which we can pose concerning man. This is precisely what overwhelms us. Their encounter occupies such a vast field because violence and language each occupy the totality of the human field.

We would be entertaining a very limited and very reassuring idea of violence if we were to reduce it to one of the two extreme forms in which it is entirely and clearly itself: on the one hand murder, that is to say, death inflicted by man on man; or, on the other hand, the strength of nature when it attacks man and cannot be tamed by him: the violence of a fire, of a hurricane, of a flood, of an avalanche, the violence of pain, of an epidemic. Between a murder and an avalanche, however, there is the whole realm of the intermediate, which is perhaps violence itself: human violence, the individual as

Translated by Joseph Bien

violence. His violence has aspects of the hurricane and of the murder: on the side of the hurricane, it is the violence of desire, of fear, and of hate; on the side of murder, it is the will to dominate the other man, the attempt to deprive him of freedom or of expression, it is racism and imperialism.

Some will say that nothing is to be gained by stretching violence so far, that in so doing we blend all the forms into a great obscurity, and the specific problems posed by oppression or revolution, or by the private hatred of one man for another, are thereby watered down. I maintain, however, that the philosopher's task here is to take the largest view of the realm of violence, from its exterior nature against which we fight, through the nature within that overwhelms us, to, finally, the will to murder that, it is said, is nourished by each consciousness in its encounter with another.

For what unifies the problem of violence is not the fact that its multiple expressions derive from one or another form that is held to be fundamental, but rather that it is language that is its opposite. It is for a being who speaks, who in speaking pursues meaning, who has already entered the discussion and who knows something about rationality that violence is or becomes a problem. Thus violence has its meaning in its other: language. And the same is true reciprocally. Speech, discussion, and rationality also draw their unity of meaning from the fact that they are an attempt to reduce violence. A violence that speaks is already a violence trying to be right: it is a violence that places itself in the orbit of reason and that already is beginning to negate itself as violence.

Such is inevitably our point of departure: violence and language measure from one end to the other as two contraries each exactly adjusted to the whole extension of the other.

One might be tempted to stop here; and, in a certain sense, we shall not go beyond this starting point, but only reach it less abstractly, more concretely. For a person cannot argue for violence without contradicting himself, since by so arguing he wants to be right and already enters the field of speech and of discussion, leaving his weapon at the door. The formal opposition of violence and language must be granted provisionally by anyone who speaks. But as soon as this has been said, one has the irresistible feeling that this formal opposition does not exhaust the problem, but rather only encircles it with a thick line surrounding emptiness.

Why is this so? Because the opposition which we understand and from which we start is not exactly the opposition of language and violence, but—according to the terminology of Eric Weil in *La Logique de la philosophie*, the echo of which was recognizable in my introduction—rather the opposition of discourse and violence, more precisely of coherent discourse and violence. No one enunciates this coherent discourse, and no one possesses it. If someone attempted to possess it, it would again be the violent person who, under the cover of fraudulently coherent speech, was attempting to make his philosophical particularity prevail.

I have just uttered a word: fraud. This word suddenly uncovers a whole somber world of falsified words which make language the voice of violence.

Violence and Language

We started from the very neat and clear antithesis of discourse and of violence, and here against the background of this formal and, in its own realm, forever insuperable opposition a sentence emerges: violence speaks. That which speaks, in relation to the meaning, is violence. We are thus brought to explore all the intermediaries of violence and of. discourse and violence.

It is quite obvious that such a problem would not have arisen if we had restricted ourselves to the anatomy of a language. It is only when we go on to a physiology of speech that such a question is capable not only of getting an answer, but more simply of being asked. Language is innocent—language meaning the tool, the code—because it does not speak, it is spoken. It is discourse which bears the problem that we are considering. It is the spoken word, not the completed, closed, and finished inventories, which bears the dialectic of meaning and of violence. It is necessary then to penetrate the dynamism of language in order to encounter the struggle for meaning in its dispute with the expression of violence. Someone must express himself—not necessarily I, Mr. So-and-So, but my people, my class, my group, etc.—in order for violence to express itself. The intention of saying something must traverse this expression in order for the aim of a meaning to be able to oppose itself to the expression of violence. There is thus in speech—but not in a language—a narrow space in which expression and the desire for meaning join and confront each other. This is where the spoken word is submitted to the most extreme tension between violence and rational meaning. Language as speech is such that it is the place where violence reaches expression at the same time that the intention of rational meaning finds support in the quest for a referent that motivates our speaking.

I would like to approach more concretely this intersection of expression—which gives voice to violence—and of the desire for meaning—which gives voice to coherent discourse. I will look for it in words, or, more exactly, in denomination, the activity of naming, which belongs not to the language itself, but to the production of speech. Some may be surprised that I am speaking here of words as belonging to the order of speech, and thus of the sentence, and not of languages or their inventories. Are not words lying quietly in our dictionaries? Certainly not. There are not yet (or there are no longer) words in our dictionaries; there are only available signs delimited by other signs within the same system by the common code. These signs become words charged with expression and meaning when they come to fruition in a sentence, when they are used and take on a use value. Of course they come from, and after usage fall back into, the lexicon; but they have real meaning only in that passing instance of discourse we call a sentence. It is then that they come onto the field of the confrontation between violence and discourse.

I would like to offer examples taken from three different spheres of our speech: politics, poetry, and philosophy. In these three spheres—which I do not in any way wish to classify hierarchically—the word, that jewel of speech, is the focus of violence and meaning.

Violence and Language

When we think of politics, we think first of all of tyranny and of revolution; this is legitimate, but it does not come close to exhausting the problem. It may even hide what is most essential. It is in the normal exercise of politics that the original intersection of violence and meaning occurs. But let us begin with tyranny. In a tyranny it is obvious that violence speaks. This is so evident that philosophers have always opposed tyranny, the extreme of power, to philosophy, which is judicious discourse. Philosophy denounces tyranny precisely because it invades philosophy's territory: language. Tyranny indeed has never been the brute and mute exercise of force. Tyranny makes its way by seduction, persuasion, and flattery; the tyrant prefers the services of the sophist to those of the executioner. Even today, especially today, Hitler rules through Goebbels. The sophist Goebbels is necessary to create the words and phrases that mobilize hate, that consolidate the society of crime, and that issue the summons to sacrifice and to death. Yes, the sophist is necessary to give violence, one need hardly say that it mobilizes speech at the moment of the new awareness. There is no revolutionary project without consciousness or without the acquisition of consciousness, therefore without articulation of meaning. But political violence is not restricted to tyranny or revolution. Step by step everything political is touched by the turgid play of meaning and violence. And undoubtedly we should speak first of meaning, for politics exists because the city exists—therefore because individuals have begun and partly succeeded in overcoming their private violence by subordinating it to a rule of law. The words of the city bear this universal mark, which is a kind of non-violence. But at the same time the community is politically united only because a force voices this form and communicates to the social body the unity of a will which makes decisions and imposes them in order to render them enforceable. Yet this great will, which is the law for individuals, is at the same time like a great irascible individual who at times speaks the language of fear, of anger, of offended dignity, of impudent boasting, that is to say, of violence. Thus the rule of law which gives form to the social body is also power, an enormous violence which elbows its way through our private violences and speaks the language of value and honor. And from here come the grand words which move crowds and sometimes lead them to death. It is through the subtle art of denomination that the common will conquers our wills; by harmonizing our private languages in a common fable of glory, it seduces our wills as well and expresses their violence, just as the juice of a fruit is expressed by squeezing.

Shall we say that such a misfortune happens only to political language? If it were to appear that the most innocent of languages—that of the poet—did not escape this double tension of meaning and violent particularity, we should then have to admit that it is all language that is thus defined and circumscribed. I hold that poetic language emerges from a certain opening that allows some aspect of Being to appear. I am here provisionally adopting Heidegger's description of speech as the submission to the prescriptions of a measure of Being to which man is originally open. This is the poet's way of giving himself up to meaning. His obedience is not submission, of which revolt or autonomy would be the contrary; his obedience resides rather in this resignation, in this "following," this letting-be. It is in this that the non-violence of discourse, of which the poetic verb is the most advanced element, consists. This is where language is least at our disposition but rather has man at its disposition.

And yet . . . and yet it is at this furthest point of non-violence that violent particularity is accumulated. How? Precisely in the impact of the word, in the strength of impact of the word; to bring being to language, according to Heidegger, is to bring being to the word. Now the word, the formation of a name, Heidegger says, "establishes a being in its Being and thus preserves it in its openness." To preserve that which is open? Here the subtle violence, which the Gospel says forces the realm, is settled and sublimated; in words, in the capture of Being by words, things become and are. An openness that is a capture, such is the poetic word, in which the violent particularity of the poet is expressed in the very moment that he abandons himself and surrenders to uncovered Being. The violent man appears at the very point where being and meaning *unfold*: in the *arrival*, in the *maturation* of the word. The poet is the violent man who forces things to speak. It is poetic *abduction*.

I will conclude this joint review of violence and discourse with a few words in philosophical language. I quite agree with Eric Weil that philosophy is entirely defined by the desire for meaning, by the choice in favor of coherent discourse. What openness is for the poet, order and coherence are for the philosopher. But this very intention and the steps that the philosopher can take in this direction risk obscuring the hidden link between discourse and the violent particularity of the philosphical individual.

There is, first of all, the violence of the initial question: the philosopher is a man seized by the specificity of a question of the *cogito*, the question of the synthetic *a priori* judgment, even the question of Being. But the philosopher always comes to thought through the narrow gap of a single question. Violence and point of departure? Violence of the point of departure? To begin is always an exercise of force, even and especially when one begins with absolute substance, as does Spinoza.

Then there is the violence also of a particular trajectory: the philosopher is one who articulates the various elements of his discourse within the horizon of a tradition, which is always a particular tradition, using words already burdened with meaning; no philosopher can totally recover the totality of his presuppositions. There can be no philosophy without presuppositions.

There is finally the violence of the always premature conclusion: philosophy exists only in books which are always a finite work of the mind. Books are always brought to a close too quickly, intercepting the process of totalization in an arbitrary termination. This is why all philosophies are particular even though everything is to be found in any great philosophy. And as I am myself one of the violent particularities, it is from my particular point of view that I perceive all these total particularities that are also particular totalities. The hard road of the "loving struggle" is the only road possible.

In concluding I would like to draw several theoretical and practical conclusions from this confrontation. The former essentially concern the notion of rational meaning, of rational discourse, which underlies all this reflection. I wish to say three things in this regard. First, this discussion has meaning only if we are able to speak of the goal of language. It is not possible to confront language and violence, nor even to set them together, without a certain project of language, without a goal. It is on this level of goals that the search for meaning gives violence an opposite. Yet is it not dangerous, even illusory, to speak of a goal of language? For who knows where it is going or what end it serves? Final causes have long been criticized by philosphers, from Descartes to Spinoza, Kant, Hegel, and Nietzsche. And yet the critique of finality, understood as a final term imposed from without on a mechanical process, does not exhaust the question of meaning, for true finality is not an end proposed from the exterior: it is the full manifestation of the orientation of a dynamism. This investigation thus forces us to return to Humboldt's view of the genesis of language as the complete manifestation of the mind, as its self-manifestation, its unfolding in plenitude. Without this vocation of language to wholly express the thinkable it is not possible to enter into a dialectic such as the one which occupies us today.

Second, to speak of rational meaning is not to speak only of the understanding of calculation or instrumental intelligence. To the contrary, any reduction of reason to understanding conspires in the end with violence. For the only thing indeed which then becomes thinkable is the organized struggle against nature. The construction of an individual or collective history becomes senseless. It is not surprising, therefore, that in this age of planning, intelligence is confronted only by the radical opposition of the beatnik or the absurdity of the aimless crime; it is only in the world of the organized struggle against nature, in a world which has reduced its project of rationality to this struggle, that pure crime—killing for the sake of killing—is conceivable.

Thirdly, when the intelligence of calculation takes hold of language itself, it produces the same effects of nonsense. To know the structures of language does not advance one a step in rational meaning. For what is in question is the meaning of discourse, not the structure of the keyboard on which it plays. The problem of language in confrontation with violence is not the problem of structure, but rather the problem of meaning, of rational meaning, that is to say, of the effort to integrate in an inclusive understanding the relationship of man to nature, of man to man, of existence and meaning, and, finally, this very relation of language and violence. The illusion by which structural intelligence is held to exhaust the understanding of language is encouraged by the belief that structural knowledge, by putting the subject between parentheses, gives freedom from the egocentric illusion. But an understanding which does not also comprehend its subject—in the double acceptation of the term, neither surrounding nor penetrating it with meaning—is a dead intelligence, a separated intelligence. Regardless of appearances, it provides no resistance to an anarchic and violent affirmation of the subject, precisely because the subject is evacuated from its field of investigation. It is not surprising that the most senseless cult of personality flourishes precisely where the most fanatical negations of the subject are uttered. Every merely instrumental intelligence, because it does not understand its own carrier, is the accomplice of violence, of the senseless affirmation of particularity. Instrumental intelligence and senseless existence are the twin orphans of the death of meaning. This is why only a work of thought in which the thinker understands himself in a meaningful history can comprehend both discourse and its opposite, violence.

But how do we live this intermediate situation between meaning and violence? To answer this question is to ask oneself what the practical implications of the initial opposition of discourse and violence are. I shall limit myself to assembling a few simple rules for the proper use of language in its confrontation with violence.

We must continue to hold it to be a formal, though empty, truth, that discourse and violence are the most fundamental opposites of human existence. Bearing continual witness to this fundamental opposition is the only condition for recognizing violence where it is and for having recourse to it when it is necessary. But he ·who has never ceased pointing violence out as the opposite of discourse will be forever safeguarded against being its apologist, against disguising it, and against believing it superseded when it has not been. Recourse to violence always must remain a limited culpability, a calculated fault; he who calls a crime a crime is already on the road to meaning and salvation.

It is necessary not only to retain as a formal truth the non-violence of discourse, but to bear witness to it as an imperative: the "Thou shalt not kill!" is always true, even when it is not applicable. He who upholds it continues to recognize the other as a rational being and attempts to honor him. Furthermore, he retains for himself the possibility of again entering into discussion with his adversary; in time of war he will never commit an act that will render peace impossible. In this manner the pressure of a morality of conviction can be maintained on the morality of responsibility. The place of the testimony of the non-violent man remains marked in history. By his out-of-place, untimely gesture the non-violent man bears witness for all men to the goal of history and of violence itself.

This second series of conclusions does not contradict the first: to recognize violence where it is, even to have recourse to violence when it is necessary, does not exclude the recognition of the place of the testimony of the non-violent man in history, for if non-violence alone belongs to the morality of conviction, on the other hand the morality of conviction can never take the place of the morality of responsibility. The dialectic of the morality of conviction and the morality of responsibility expresses our position even in the interspace of discourse and violence.

Violence and Language

The third rule for the proper use of language concerns what I will call the non-violent practice of discourse itself. Violence in discourse consists in the claim that a single one of its modalities exhausts the realm of speech. To be non-violent in discourse is to respect the plurality and diversity of languages. It is to leave the modes of discourse in their proper places: here the language of calculation and all the languages of understanding, there rational meaning and its project of totalization, in another place mythical interpellation and prophetic language, which open man to the very origin of the meaning which he does not have at his disposition but which has him at its disposition.

Respect for the multiplicity, diversity, and hierarchy of languages is the only way for men to work towards rational meaning.

PART II

THE CHRISTIAN AND SOCIETY

5

YE ARE THE SALT OF THE EARTH

THE DIFFICULTY OF SALTING

THE FIRST THING I WANT TO SAY IS HOW GLAD I AM TO be alive at a time when Christian preaching has rediscovered all the dimensions of the Christian message: historical, geographical, social and political, a time when Christians feel concerned for everything that happens to men. "Nothing human is foreign to me" has now become a Christian slogan, not merely a Stoic one. In the light of the Christian hope we have discovered afresh the *fullness* of the Christianity of which St. Augustine wrote in *The City of God*, when he traced the history of the Roman Empire—its decadence, the rise of the barbarians, the invasion of Africa. After several centuries during which Christians have been preoccupied with the inner life and personal salvation we are discovering afresh what is meant by "the salt of the earth." We are discovering that the salt is made for salting, the light for illuminating, and that the Church exists for the sake of those outside itself. Let us be glad that this is happening at a time when the Church has less power and when Christians are in a minority; this gives the Church greater opportunity for exercising a prophetic role.

Now I am going to ask you a number of questions which confront those who recognize themselves to be the salt of the earth, those who say, "We are the salt of the earth, we realize it; but what can we do about it?" Or, "I am the salt, I should like to fall into the soup, but the soup-tureen is covered up."

It is this situation that I want to discuss: the difficult position of the Christian Church in the world. I hope thus to give it an impetus which will enable it to tackle obstacles and to emerge more mature after considering the problem. I want to examine the obstacles to action encountered by the Church in the world today, and to consider what technique it should adopt.

Of course, there are some obstacles within the Church itself; we know them only too well: the inertia of the churches, their preoccupation with their traditional message, their failure to face the struggles and hopes of modern people, and the way in which they sometimes seek escape through liturgy or personal piety.

But this kind of resistance within the Church would not be so tenacious if it were not allied with resistance outside. It is true that, apart from the people to whom St. John alludes when he says that "Light . . . was in the world . . . and the world knew him not" (John 1:10), there is an opaqueness inherent in the very nature of *action in modern societies* against which good will is powerless. As you know,

every problem—housing, underdevelopment, un-
employment, the movement for liberating colored
peoples, the rise of nationalism in Asia and Africa,
and others—has become so highly technical that
people are discouraged from tackling it. These
technical intricacies present a reef upon which the
enthusiasm of young people may be shattered.

THE DIFFICULTY OF TAKING ACTION IN THE SPHERE OF POLITICS

Basic changes in society are bound to affect
politics. Politics exist because the *State* exists,
i.e., a body which organizes the great collectives,
takes decisions on the highest level, organizes the
community as a whole, and has the monopoly of the
use of force. Our good will comes up against this
fact: that if we are to change things we must influence
the power of the State. That is politics. "Politics
may be defined as the sum of all the efforts made
to participate in power, and to influence the distribution of power." (Max Weber.)

This difficulty has existed in every period of
history, but in modern societies it has assumed
colossal proportions. Is the Church going to enter
this struggle for power? In former times the answer
was "yes." Today, if the Church is not to take part
in politics like a political party, how is it to influence the State? How can it endeavour to influence
the political power? Today, this question has assumed
considerable proportions, because the State has not
merely developed into a gigantic institution, but also
into a secular institution; it is normal that the State

should be non-confessional owing to its technical nature.

Consequently politics—as a form of competition for power—is officially detached from any religious affirmation. This brings us to the strange paradox which baffles every young Christian: in order to manifest my faith I have to act in the world; but in order to act in the world I have to put my faith on one side.

It is even more inevitable that faith should become neutralized in political action as soon as that action ceases to be episodic and becomes militant or professional. This means joining an organization which has its own laws of functioning, and its own standards of efficiency. If the Christian is to influence the masses he is obliged to appeal to their emotions in some striking manner; he will have to resort to outrageous simplifications, to appeal to their personal interests, to play off one group against another, perhaps even to invoke hatred of one another. One may well ask how the Church can give its message of truth and love in a sphere which is so complex, so disconcerting and often so scandalous as politics.

THE AMBIGUOUS WORLD OF THE IDEOLOGIES

If the Christian wants to keep out of the political sphere, he can act on a second level: he can act through movements of public opinion which make certain claims and hold revolutionary ideals. These movements exercise ideological pressure. We may take as an example the revolutionary literature of the 19th century.

Ye Are the Salt of the Earth

This literature has had a tremendous influence in history. It undoubtedly started a struggle for power, but in the first place it was militant criticism: it criticized money, property, class distinction, imperialism, colonialism. Its method of attack was essentially ideological. This power of criticism was combined with protests against suffering and appeals to an ideal of reconciliation among men. All this has been changing the face of history for the last century. This revolutionary literature has resulted not only in the appearance of new parties, it has also influenced the action of the trade unions, and has affected groups of opinion, schools of thought, and literary works.

What problems does this ideological action raise for us?

Essentially it raises the problem of the militant ideologies. Nothing great is achieved in history without *passion*, and the most powerful passions are those which have been rationalized by the ideologies. But the relation between the great revolutionary ideologies and the Christian message is a very strange one: they are very close to it, and at the same time entirely different from it. The superficial resemblance between them is just as disturbing as the apparent antithesis between them. In fact they are very close to the Christian message when they attack the churches for the conservative attitude they have adopted for the last three centuries, and when they denounce the hypocrisy of a piety which is divorced from justice and love. In this they seem to echo the great prophets, the Sermon on the Mount, or the social message of the apostles. But these ideologies are very far from the Christian message even when they most resemble it, for instance, in their belief in the redemption of history and the reconciliation of men, for the simple reason that this redemption and this reconciliation do not pass through Jesus Christ but through the sacrifice of a social class, which is (as it were) a purely human and collective Christ. This type of humanized Christology can be heard running like an undertone through all the revolutionary ideologies of the 19th century.

Wherein lies the difficulty of Christian action?

One may think, "There is no difficulty; I will accept what is Christian in the ideologies and ignore what is anti-Christian." But this is more easily said than done. Ideologies put up strong resistance against such distinctions; their whole effectiveness lies in their being swallowed whole. One is tempted to say that illusions are the only things that are effective in history, and that it was these impure mixtures which succeeded in liberating the slaves. And the Christian always runs the risk of looking like the gentleman who analyzes and blunts the revolutionary weapon.

THE DIFFICULTIES OF SOCIAL ACTION

If the Christian wants to keep out of politics, and also to avoid action through movements with an ideological basis, there is still a vast field of *social action* before him. Such action is purely therapeutic and educative: schemes for slum clearance and housing, attempts to combat alcoholism, prostitution, and others.

Ye Are the Salt of the Earth

In this sphere there may seem to be no difficulty; one seems to be on safe ground; there is no more violence, no more insincerity, and the Christian may feel that he can do something really effective. But precisely here we are faced by a much subtler way in which the world excludes the light of the Christian message. Social therapy and the methods whereby society combats the great scourges of modern life have assumed a form which is increasingly secular and technical, this being the price paid for organization and efficiency. This technical approach is derived from industry, where organizing and planning made their first conquests. The systematic division of labor has enabled man to conquer the world. This same technique is now applied to all human relations, with even greater severity. There is something relentless about this trend, which must be accepted as one of the factors of modern life. The State was the first to benefit by this through an administration, i.e., an executive body, which extended over the whole community like a big factory, in accordance with the laws of rational organization. This trend to organization, which is derived from the industrial world and has passed into the administration of the State, has spread like wildfire. All enterprises, even small, private ones, obey this inflexible law of growing complexity, whereby human relations become more and more impersonal. If he is to give effective help to someone, the Good Samaritan of today has to isolate himself more and more from those he wants to help, through a whole gamut of administrative machinery. The spirit of all these bodies is therefore bound to become abstract and de-humanized, while at the same time it is the condition of their effectiveness. In the societies where planning is most highly developed, for instance the people's democracies, this problem takes the form of bureaucracy.

The Christian is faced by a dilemma: he would like to love his neighbors without intermediary, as man to man; it is characteristic of love that it is addressed to one irreplaceable person whom Jesus defined as follows (in the words of Pascal): "It was for thee that I shed this drop of my blood." An administration does not speak like that. In order to do something for a certain person, the administration has to cease regarding him as a person and turn him into a "case," with a Social Welfare number, entitled to a priority file, etc. . . .

Moreover, the driving power behind this social therapy no longer seems to have any connection with the proclamation of God's Kingdom. All these bodies tend to become mere machinery for correcting the imperfect functioning of the social structure. For instance, the earnings of productive persons are diverted for the benefit of non-productive persons. (These two sociological categories, "productive" and "non-productive," do not correspond in any way with the categories of Christian love.)

This situation presents a real problem to the militant Christian who wonders if he can introduce a Christian gesture in the world. Whatever he does runs the risk of becoming more and more impersonal, more and more emptied of its prophetic substance.

It is the same paradox that we spoke of before: in order to manifest the love of Christ in this world, must it be neutralized into action which is lay, secular and technical? *Must the salt lose its savor, in order that the world may be salted?*

THE SALT MUST KEEP ITS SAVOR

I have not collected these problems just for the pleasure of worrying you, worrying myself, or cultivating a sense of defeatism. My purpose is to assist reflection, to develop a naïve enthusiasm into a mature, resolute form of commitment. We will now examine in turn each of the three spheres that we have just mentioned. But the general tone of my reply will be as follows:

We have to accept the conditions for action as they present themselves. The first sign of Christian hope is to believe that something can always be done in every situation. When the Gospel says that the Church has the promises of eternal life, this means that the message of truth and love can take root at any period of history.

"Ye are the salt of the earth." As we just said, this is a fact, a situation resulting in an order. It is not a memory of the past; it is an ever present condition. We therefore have to accept the rules of the games as they stand, and not dream of playing some other game.

In face of the complex, technical character of all action, the first point to be emphasized is this: it is the strict duty of the young Christian to *recognize* the machinery for social action, the rules governing social therapy. It is his duty to inform himself and to train himself. In the world in which we live, the Christian must not be an amateur. He must make himself competent with the devotion of a soldier. The message of love must be transmitted through the modern channels offered by the world as it is; it must not lose itself in vague regrets or protests against the rules of the game.

I will now indicate three permanent functions of Christian love in the sphere of social action.

I think the first function of Christian charity in the sphere of social action is a *corrective* one. It works in the opposite way to the impersonal methods of mutual aid. Love is a personal thing, lying at the very heart of the technical projects which make it impersonal. You say, "Social security tends to make human relations abstract." Well, how can direct personal contacts be established within this modern system? It is from within the system itself that we have to struggle against its tendency to become dehumanized; but we have to seize the opportunities inherent in this system. Love is that tact, that flair for always detecting the personal significance of anything that tends to become a "case." We have to discover how these techniques can be molded and adapted in each particular instance. We must do a lot of thinking about the problem of bureaucracy, and about the struggle against bureaucracy; we must realize that behind this technical problem lies a spiritual question. But this problem must be tackled with the resources of law, of administration and technical planning in order to make social therapy more adaptable, more flexible to meet each particular case.

To put it briefly, the purpose of Christian love in the 20th century is to maintain this constant tension between the final object of social therapy (who is a person) and the methods (which are a system). The temptation which faces any organization is to regard itself as an end in itself, to function in a vacuum. Our service will express itself in vigilant care to protect what is personal within the organization that we have set up.

Precisely because social therapy is applied, it tends to become blind to new forms of injustice. All social therapy contains a conservative element, rather than a prophetic one. The Gospel says, "The poor ye have always with you." Christian love consists in seeking out the fresh forms of poverty which occur at any period. Just as we are dealing with one of its recognized forms, poverty changes its aspect.

Thus all contemporary societies have a golden rule: productivity. Both in America and in the Soviet Union, this is based on enormous differences in salary. The whole struggle of the 18th century for political equality has become ineffectual owing to this pitiless law of modern labor based on a hierarchy of salaries. This hierarchy is one of the conditions of output and in the long run creates wealth for all. But, in the meantime, we see that modern society, through the very form of work and organization, creates fresh categories of underprivileged people who are crushed by the system without being noticed. Social therapy tends to protect the categories which are largest and best organized. Many other categories are left to their fate; the organization of society itself produces people who are failures, who cannot adapt themselves.

Another example is the problem of old people. This problem will become more and more terrible in modern societies, partly owing to the fact that people live longer, and partly to the fact that people are forced to retire too soon. A further aggravating circumstance is that, since societies change more rapidly than formerly, an elderly man is psychologically less adapted to life than formerly, and feels more out of things. This is a new form of poverty, not necessarily due to lack of money but to psychological causes. While the amount of work done in the world is constantly increasing, there is also more leisure, empty leisure, in which boredom tends to take the place of suffering and hard work.

On the social plane we must therefore be on the watch to discover which of our neighbors are among the new poor.

I will illustrate this by one example: the problem of hunger which is one of the signs of the maladjustment of world society. The difference between rich and poor is constantly increasing, because the rich part of the world is getting richer much more rapidly than the poor part. But the rich part of the world shuts its eyes to the poverty of the poor part. This problem is becoming crucial for France. During the last three or four years growing sections of our population have passed into the category of the rich, and this has blinded them to the poverty of the world. Certain governing classes of the proletariat are won over by this spirit, so that the division tends to form more and more between Europe and America on the one hand, and Africa and Asia on the other. For instance, the Communist Party has had the greatest difficulty in mobilizing the working classes to do something for Algeria. The reason for this complete failure is that today the French working class is swinging over to support the interests of Europe, as opposed to those of Africa and Asia.

In order to retain our sympathy for the misfortunes of men, we therefore need to have a worldwide view of the problems. Christian love today must direct its attention towards the great world questions—not merely devote itself to details and individuals. Its vigilance consists no longer in service but in revolution, because it certainly involves sacrifices.

The recent works of certain economists show that the wealth of the world will have to be redistributed through gifts. In order to adjust the balance, wealth will have to be taken from the rich and given to the poor; the cards will have to be reshuffled. I think it is one of the basic tasks of the Christian Church to show the "haves" that they must give to the "have-nots" on a world-wide scale. This will probably take the form of transfers (entirely free from political interests) through international loan organizations which have nothing to do with the politics of the great powers. Such a task demands the very best of which we are capable. But in order to launch the project and to strengthen the desire and the good will to carry it out, Christian motives will be *indispensable*; for we cannot feel the need for such a project unless we lay aside our collective egoism and get a different world outlook. I call this the revolutionary influence of Christian love.

Thus love makes human relationships more per-

sonal in a society which tends to make them mechanical; but love also requires us to include the
whole world in our projects for mutual aid, when
they tend to restrict themselves to the big collective
egoisms.

You remember the difficulty: the real influences
in history have been the great ideologies, which are
in some ways very similar to the Christian Gospel,
but in others entirely different. Here the salt of
the earth is *truth.* In many opinions the Christian
believes, with St. John, that *"the truth shall make
you free."* We should let ourselves be cut in pieces
rather than deny that. We can never admit that
humanity needs doping with illusions or myths. It is
precisely our respect for man which prevents us
from thinking that he needs any kind of opiate:
human beings are worthy of better things.

We believe that man is capable of truth, and that
the truth can set him free. That is Christian optimism
and we must never abandon it. We must have the
courage to stake all on the belief that it is possible
to influence history without having recourse to myths,
without believing in automatic progress, or in the
innocence of the proletariat or in national sovereignty.
Since it is the truth which sets us free, I think the
Christian ought to proclaim that a total and totalitarian
ideology is useless, and that we do not need a new
religion. The Christian is convinced that the claims
of the big ideologies and their essential falsehoods
have been the source of fresh forms of violence in
the world for the past century, and still are.

118

For instance, torture had almost disappeared in the 18th century—a period which recognized the relativity of political doctrines. Today torture has reappeared, owing to the pretentious doctrines of fascism, Stalinism, and the imperialist ideology of the white race.

The Christian will therefore be an idol smasher, an iconoclast, a profaner of ideologies. It is his function to restore truth to its rightful place, and thus to reveal the secular dimensions of history. It is a task of purification and healing.

People will object, "That is negative. How can we do something positive?" I should like to give two examples to show that this smashing of ideologies has a liberating effect.

Every ideology contains a power of falsification; at a given moment—in order to preserve itself—the ideology has to falsify the truth, to falsify documents, to falsify history, as was done at the time of Stalin. It is a sort of refusal to face the truth. When confronted by this power of falsehood, I think the function of the Christian is to return to the facts, to the positive meaning of the facts.

Here is an example which concerns us directly and which I ask you to take as a problem of conscience: the problem of the war in Algeria. I will say at once that the Christian has no ready-made solution just because he is a Christian. But I think he has a special function as a Christian, whatever his opinions may be (though I fully admit that we may differ considerably about the solutions). I think all Christians should agree about one thing: we should not be afraid to speak out, and especially to denounce

119

all use of torture, as such, without exaggerating the facts or concealing them. I think the very first essential is to purify the situation through truth. And telling the truth means asking what is the meaning of this war—not only its cost, but also its purpose. It means asking whether there is any connection between torture and the revolutionary character of the insurrection. After that we may differ about the solution of the problem. But we shall have a basis of truth on which to take our decision, as Christians.

The ideologies could not survive in history, in spite of the falsehoods they proclaim, were it not for the ideals behind them.

I will take another example in the same field. The French Republic is based on a conception of law, of basic freedoms, of personal security, independence of justice, and correct procedure in making accusations and arrests. That is its ideal. But if that is what France professes, let her live up to it all the time, and in every situation. If that is what we oppose to the arbitrary power of Stalinism, then let us be true to it, not only when it leads us towards the right but also when it leads us towards the left. After that we must ask ourselves to what point we can carry on a war whose insurrectional character excludes the application of legal measures. After that, let us talk.

The spirit of truth is a desire for facts—the facts which are concealed by ideologies—and the return to the ideal which ideologies use merely for window-dressing, to justify themselves. That is why I am proud that Christians are seeking this spirit of truth, the truth which shall make France pure and free.

CHRISTIAN SALT IN POLITICS

In the first place we must stress the seriousness of political action. It is true that political action is open to tremendous criticism; it is influenced by passion, it gives opportunity for many base feelings and resentments, the desire for power, and the craving for show and influence.

The saving factor about politics is that they have to involve *responsibility*. In the true sense politics is an activity undertaken by responsible men. They are responsible because the public interest and the permanent trend of the nation is ultimately involved. Politics finally becomes respectable because of its decisive, indelible influence on society.

Moralists, philosophers, preachers are not responsible for what they do. The politician, on the other hand, is responsible for the consequences of his actions, because his problem is constantly to decide what is feasible in practice, not merely what is desirable.

That is why the law of politics is never the law of purity, the law of all or nothing, as the law of religious conscience is. The religious conscience says: "If thou art not perfect in every respect, thou art not perfect at all." Politics is never subject to this law; its achievements can never be more than relatively good. That is why the politician is faced by a terrible problem; it is not the problem of maintaining his innocence, but that of *limiting his culpability*.

Being the salt of the earth means that the Church must maintain the tension between a morality of absolute right and wrong (the morality of the Gospel) and the morality of what is feasible in practice (the morality of politics). The Church must maintain this tension almost to breaking point.

It would be the greatest hypocrisy if the Christian were to insist on introducing the absolute claims of the Sermon on the Mount directly and brutally into politics, ignoring the tension between such absolute claims and the relative, inadequate possibilities of political action.

For example, the problem of non-violence. From the political point of view the immediate acceptance of the principle of non-violence is a wild dream which might even result in increasing the violence and disorder in the world owing to its disregard for the consequences. The purist will either refuse to take any action at all, or else become a terrorist, when the moment actually arises. This is one of the problems raised by Sartre in the second part of *Le diable et le bon Dieu*. At a certain moment the purist will be seized by a dream which may lead him to say: for the first and last time I must exercise violence, a violence which will destroy terrorism for the sake of the Christian absolute.

Being the salt of the earth in politics means maintaining the constant pressure of moral conviction upon the politician's sense of responsibility, maintaining the pressure of non-violence upon legitimate violence. It seems to me that the Church in the 20th century is nearer than ever before to recognizing the rules of this game and playing it fairly. For it is just abandoning another game: the illusion that it can play a direct political role itself as an independent political power. The Church is slowly abandoning that attitude. Even today, however, all the churches still have far more political influence than is warranted by their religious faith. There is a kind of dishonesty and hypocrisy about this. In France, for instance, barely one-fifth of the population are really Catholics, nevertheless the political influence of the Church extends over half the electorate. This illusion that we are still living in a Christian era is a formidable hypocrisy which poisons the political life of the West: the so-called "Christian" parties, "Christian" trade unions, and the influence of clericalism form a heritage which it is not easy to get rid of.

In my opinion, political action undertaken by the Church risks prolonging the death throes of Christendom as a political factor, and of clericalism. These death throes have a demoralizing effect on Christians and also on non-Christians, driving them to cynicism, amoralism and despair.

When it emerges from this illusion, the Church will be able to give light once more to all men—no longer as a power, but as a prophetic message. A prophetic message for the State, and for the political sphere, is by no means a condemnation of them but justifies them within certain limits. And by imposing limitation on them, this message fixes their just rights. It may be said without fear that only the Church knows what the State is, because it knows what the State is *not*. The Church alone knows that the State is the legitimate magistrate entrusted with the sword, simply in order that societies may survive. The State itself does not know this. It is not there to save humanity, but to ensure that it shall continue. The Church alone knows that the problem of politics consists in restricting the use of force to this task of survival. In this sense it may be said that the Church justifies the State and politics, up to a certain point.

And because its message is one of good news for the State, the Church can from time to time say "no"—but then it is a "no" related to certain definite facts; for instance, the Confessing Church in Germany had to reject the anti-semitism of the State; and in 1957 the Church of France had to reject the use of torture. But this refusal, this prophetic message urging the State to be on its guard, should be given only in very exceptional cases; it should always be protected by the insight of the daily acceptance of the State, as the power indicated by the apostles when they recommended Christians to make intercession for the authorities.

In conclusion, I should simply like to say that there must always be a Church of sacrament and prayer, to keep these tensions alive. It would be a complete mistake to regard personal piety and commitment within the Church as opposed to commitment in the world.

6

FAITH AND CULTURE

ALL THE PROBLEMS WHICH STILL IN THE TWENTIETH century arise when the preaching of the Cross of Christ comes up against secular culture centered on science, the arts, ethics, and politics are the consequences of an event which had incalculable consequences: this event was the success which the Christian mission had in Greece on the original soil of Western culture. That the Gospel burst the walls of the synagogue, that it spread first into the land of Parmenides, Pythagoras, and Plato, and not somewhere else—not, for example, into Egypt or India or Africa—that is an event which we may treat either as a simple accident, even a tragic mistake, or as the most significant of the cultural events in our history. This encounter, this mission, this cultural grafting will seem to be a dreadful mistake if we decide that the Cross of Christ confounds and shatters all culture, and that every attempt to reinterpret the Gospel in terms of Greek culture, and conversely every attempt to remold the courses of this culture on the basis of Christian preaching, are blasphemous and vain. But then the Christian must undo his own history, make St. Paul retrace his footsteps in Asia, and reduce his faith to a synagogue heresy.

And yet it is said: "I will destroy the wisdom of the wise, and will bring to nothing the understanding of the prudent." And it is written: "for after that, in the wisdom of God, the world by wisdom knew not God, it pleased God by the foolishness of preaching to save them that believe."

Yes, that is said and written. But it is starting from this very saying that the original fatherland of culture was conquered and a "third man" was born: a man whom the Covenant of Israel could not contain nor produce, for this man is *par excellence* a Gentile, but a man whom the Greek educational system could not have produced or contained either, for foolishness had broken its bounds. This "third man," this cultivated Christian, this believing Greek, is ourselves. It is the charter of life, the system of thought of this "third man" that we must incessantly seek for and rediscover. This charter and this system seem to me to consist in a rhythm, a paradox in which a task of breaking away and a task of reconciliation ceaselessly oppose each other and add to each other.

THE VANITY OF MAN'S ATTEMPTED INDEPENDENCE

I belong to a generation which learned afresh during the years 1930-35 the meaning of sharp edges, of theological accuracy, of specificity on Christian preaching. That was a good thing; it was

126

necessary even when it was not enough and was only the reverse side of a liberating and constructive message. And if by chance the word of reconciliation which we are more inclined to accentuate today brought us back to the easygoing confusions, the vague syncretisms that we have painfully learned to dissolve, there would have to be sounded again the same note of attack which comes from a Gospel which lacks "wisdom of words, lest the Cross of Christ should be made of none effect."

But we have learned to understand this task of breaking away better by relating it to a task of reconciliation. What does the Word of God condemn? Is it the humanity of man? Is the "Jealousy" of God that of the god of Greek tragedy, Nemesis, which will not suffer man to be a creator of things, of ideas, of works, of institutions? Does God set a boundary, a finite limit to the cultural adventure of learning, of the arts, of morality, of politics? Then the God of Jesus Christ is not the God who became man, who assumed the humanity of man; he only assumed it to make it impossible and to render guilty human existence as such.

We have to learn over and over again that the Word of God is a word of death, not in relation to the foundation *intention* of the humanity of man, but in regard to its historical *pretensions*. In short, we must exercise the difficult "discernment" between what humanizes man and what makes him divine in a perverse way. The word of the serpent, "Ye shall be as gods," indicates the meaning of the discernment: it is not the infinite extension of human genius which is questioned by the folly of

the Cross, but its claim to totality, to self-suffi-
ciency, to being for its own sake, in short, its "passion for the limit." This passionate moment is not
the original impetus, the historical substance of
man, but the index of vanity, the Nothing which makes
him mad and secretly sanctions the death of God.
The "wisdom" which the Cross confounds and an-
nihilates is nothing but this Nothing, this vanity of
man in the clutches of this passion for the limit.

For this reason the task of a theologically based
criticism of culture consists in recognizing what kind
of "vanity" and idolatry characterizes the human
enterprise in our day. For example, the point at
which modern science goes over into pretension and
vanity is certainly not in the building up of a mathe-
matics and of a mathematical physics, but in the
scientist's belief that the universe as a whole can
be reduced to a reality of a physico-mathematical
type. This carrying of everything to the limit—or
to a system—produces a real mutation accompanied
by passionate feeling in comparison with the reasonable enterprise of mathematicizing nature; it is the
"vanity" of scientism grafted on to the scientific
vocation.

The same thing is true of the alienation which
affects the ethical conscience when it presumes
to invent good and evil from the beginning, to create
values, and to proceed to a veritable establishing
by man of his own humanity. The "vanity" travesties
the legitimate moral vocation of man: it is true
that man inaugurates every special order, every
concrete sense of justice, every historical discernment of value, but this invention is only possible

on the assumption of a liberty intimately orientated and internally related by a principle of legitimacy: man is not the absolute beginning of the valid and the non-valid under pain of failure to distinguish the executioner from the victim; it is because he is in his origins linked with a principle (however formal and bare it may be) of ethical validity that he invents concrete values, but within a realm of value which determines his will on primordial grounds. The movement from the ethical inventory to the radical creation of the very demand for ethical validity constitutes a second example of carrying everything to the limit and of the system wherein the same "vanity" of human wisdom is to be recognized.

These two examples are enough to give an idea of the "discerning of spirits" in which the task of breaking away consists.

It is tempting to believe that one can work out an economy of this emendation of the human, this stripping off of vanity. We are very ready to believe that the heritage of "humanism" is a treasury of "neutral" truths and values in the face of the preaching of the Cross, and that it is easy to "add" the dimension of faith to that of "culture" as one may add a storey to an unfinished building. This illusion is not unjustified; there is no obstacle indeed to our completing a mathematical or an ethical culture by an authentic religious life. The illusion comes from our not considering the living movement of culture, but her abstract products in some way "neutralized" by long use. But behind these products which have come into public consumption, behind these sedimented deposits, we must find the moment of original creation; this return from the "sedimented" to the "original" reveals anew the man of the limit. As soon as I restore the creative movement of the Greek man, of the man of the twelfth century, of the man of the Renaissance, of the man of the eighteenth century, I find again the "pathos" of the great humanisms of history; from this fire fell the cold cinders which we mistake today for an authentic culture and which are only the deposit or the legacy of our civilization. The enigma of history is that no human grandeur appeared without being reinforced by this "pathos"; as though this grandeur were henceforth indistinguishable from its culpability. That is why we shall never work out the economy of a criticism of culture: this is the equivalent in our intellectual life of the putting off of the old man.

THE TASK OF RECONCILIATION

And yet it is impossible to stop at a theology of breaking away. The Gospel is in every respect a ministry of reconciliation: of man with man, of Greek with Jew, and finally of oneself with oneself. It is neither possible nor desirable that man should remain divided and torn. Christianity is not the preaching of an internal warfare, of anguish and insoluble contradictions, it is a preaching of unity and peace.

That is why denunciations, ruptures, and oppositions are still only the beginning and re-beginning of a "sanctification" of the understanding.

This reconciliation is fundamentally possible. For two reasons: first because the intention of the human enterprise rather than its pretensions—that is, the intention to know, to be able, to will, in short the positive in man—expresses the creative intention of God for man. God, in creating man, creates his creators; all creation, fundamentally, participated in this original gift of humanity to man. We do not believe that man had to steal his humanity from a jealous God or that man should be condemned to be stirred up in the fire in order to become man. This is the tragic God presupposed by the modern critics of Christianity, Marxists or existentialists, when they enclose all our culture in the alternative: either a God who is object, essence, value, who condemns man to sleep in ignorance and obedience, or else a man subject, transcendent, creating values, who begins his reign by the murder of a jealous God. Our God is a God-Act, a God-Gift, who makes man a creator in his turn in the measure in which he receives and is willing to receive the gift of being free. That is why faith condemns nothing of what "is" but only the "vain," the "pseudo," the "nothing" which swells the passion for the limit.

The task of a criticism of culture is to strip man of his pretensions in order to lay bare—to discover and to reveal in the proper sense—the original destination of man; the "no" of criticism is only the reverse side of a creator's "yes."

This "yes" which we must rediscover in the Genesis, in the Origin, is also the "yes" of the End, of the Promise, of the Apocalypse. The treasure of the nations on the Last Day will be laid at the feet of the Lamb: which means that the Kingdom only comes like a thief, by breaking and entering, like a

Divine surprise, because it accomplishes, recapitulates, activates, and perfects. It is in the theology of the Kingdom that breaking away and reconciliation come to terms. But I only come to think of pruning through growth; of suppression through achievement; of "stripping off" through "totalization." Omega is as much "yes" as Alpha: He spoke and it was done. He speaks and it will be. After that promise man is free with the glorious liberty of the sons of God: free from idols, he is set free for every adventure of science, art, morals and politics.

Thus did St. Paul with regard to the pagan values of the Hellenistic world; when he named the "fruit of the Spirit" it was hospitality, gentleness, temperance, the justice of poets and philosophers,—the Greek educational ideals—that he assumes, baptizes, and transfigures. This is our task, too, in relation to the values of learning, feeling, and action which man has developed in the course of his spiritual adventure.

An opposite illusion to the one mentioned above tends to endow this task of revision and sanctification with secular values. This illusion is no longer that of the natural man; it is on the contrary that of the Church-man; the Christian Church brings with it a clerical "pathos" which makes it treat as rebellion or impiety everything that a man does "expansively"; modern culture, we must not forget, proceeded from the breaking of the false medieval synthesis between theology and secular learning; man has only been able to enter into possession of his multiple potentialities by an act of rebellion of which all our culture bears the scar; science and arts, ethics and politics, could only unfold their own problematics, their own crisis, by breaking the clerical "pathos" and opposing their "pathos" of the limit. From the point of view of the ecclesiastical totality which is today in ruins all culture has a negative aspect. Today, again, man only takes possession of himself through the rebellion of the great nineteenth century atheisms. Here the "discerning of spirits" is most valuable. It consists not only in discerning "vanity" without the pretensions of man and his culture; it consists also in discerning the "Yes" of the beginning and the Promise in the apparently vehement negations of modern man. For through the passion for the limit beyond all vanity, man unfolds the *magisterium* which was entrusted to him at the beginning and of which the works are tested in the last day through fire.

7

FROM NATION TO HUMANITY: TASK OF CHRISTIANS

THE TIME IN WHICH WE LIVE IS ONE OF PLANETARY consciousness. This fact, recent as it is, is a general one. All civilizations recognize that they are part of a single human experience.

But at the same time, we feel acutely that the road leading from the nation to humanity is blocked by obstacles of all kinds: structural obstacles resulting from the very form which our historical experience has taken, and conjunctural obstacles resulting from the circumstances of world politics in the past few decades.

Planetary consciousness, structural obstacles, and conjunctural obstacles form a unitary constellation, which first calls for an analysis and then an acceptance of responsibility.

Translated by Hoke Robinson

From Nation to Humanity: Task of Christians

PART ONE

DIFFICULT PROGRESS

Planetary consciousness

Modern man's world consciousness differs completely from what could have been experienced in other epochs: the ancient world, the medieval world, or even the classical age. The civilized world was then represented as a great island surrounded by barbarians, foreigners, the uncivilized. Even the 18th century, which conceived the first project of *perpetual peace* (the title of a large number of essays, of which Kant's is the most famous), pictured this peace essentially as a compact among civilized states and nations.

We are certainly the first historical epoch which takes a global view of its destiny. The elements of this planetary consciousness are easy to discover.

There is first of all a *technico-scientific subfoundation*. In respect to it one can scarcely overemphasize the importance of the adventure of world domination, which is experienced with different degrees of clarity by all men, and is felt in their history as a determining factor of unification. Of course, there was always a technology, but ours is the first civilization for which technology is a dominant category which suffices to characterize the epoch. This consciousness of belonging to a single enterprise of scientific and technological conquest diffuses and radiates, beginning with the core of material technology, until it forms an ever more complete matrix of the human phenomena

135

cutting across demography, political economy, political science, the technologies of management and administration, the social sciences, and others. All these forms of technico-scientific adventure have a universal, or better, universalist character.

To this first factor of technological order may be added a *strictly political factor.* Planetary consciousness has unfortunately advanced by means of violence, of war. What we have called world-wide, before peace, is war. The last two wars have been seen by the aggregate of men not as a local phenomenon but as a world-wide event. Here war has taken the lead over peace. Even today, the atomic peril is felt by all as a danger which affects humanity as a whole and even, for the first time, affects its biological capital, its capacity to survive. The possibility that history will stop gives us suddenly the feeling that history is one; hence the planetary character of contemporary politics conceived as a survival operation. Even today it is considered a criterion of the political maturity and responsibility of heads of state to know if they are capable of conceiving politics according to two contrary objectives: on the one hand to assure the existence and the strength of their state, and at the same time to protect world peace in such a way that humanity survives. Thus many of the doubts entertained today about Chinese politics are bound up with this point: does this country regard as equally important the defense of its own patrimony and the safeguarding of the peace?

Decolonization is equally an accelerating factor in the grasping of planetary consciousness. The ap-

proaching (at least, nominal) independence of at
least 120 nation-states is an event of some magnitude.
Even if they do not have among them one real
equality, even if actually these independences are
fictive, this fiction itself is a psychological and
political fact of some magnitude. As Paul VI said
at the UN: "Here you are not equals, but you make
yourselves equals." The abstract procedure which
consists in giving equally a voice to Gabon and to
the Soviet Union is indicative of this grasp of consciousness. Thus we form the idea of a human kind
of politics, able for the first time to give a concrete
meaning to the idea of those philosophers according
to whom humanity is not a species, in the sense of
animals, but a history, that is to say, a united history.

As a result, today the foreign policy of every
country has become the domestic policy of humanity.

Structural obstacles

But the plan of a united humanity has progressed
beyond the reality for reasons of two kinds which I
have placed under the headings of structural obstacles and conjunctural obstacles. These obstacles
make it difficult to give an enduring political form
to what we have nevertheless begun to experience
as a single destiny. Certainly the obstacles are also
fulcrums; they include gaps and offer avenues of
attack. They suffice nevertheless to give to this
planetary consciousness the aspect of an unhappy
consciousness, afflicted with contradictions and
distortions.

I shall speak first of the most ancient and enduring
obstacles: the *structural* obstacles which result

from the form into which humanity up until now has poured its history, namely the *nation-state*. (The stress, however, should perhaps be placed more on the conjunctural obstacles than on the structural obstacles.)

In speaking of nation-states we establish perhaps too quickly two distinct factors which coincide only in the old countries of Europe such as France, England, and more recently Italy, Germany, and others. States and nations do not, however, include exactly the same reality and do not each represent the same order of obstacles to mondialization.[1] The State is a juridical obstacle; the nation is an organic obstacle.

If today we can only imagine a world state with difficulty, this is because of the fundamental characteristics the *State* has been seen to possess especially since the 16th century in Europe. This State has become for us the form of power at the interior of finite historical communities; it is the agent of a historical community, the mode of organization which makes it capable of making decisions; it is essentially a capacity for decision in a finite community. To this, its principal characteristic, is added that of the unconditional exercise of violence, which functions only within the geographical limits of that state's sovereignty. But we have yet to discover how decision and force could be exercised in some structure other than in this limited, finite, and closed form which is sovereignty. In this respect the diversity of constitutional forms is less an obstacle than the fundamental fact of sovereignty. This fact is responsible for our not knowing how to move from the multiplicity of sovereign states to a universal state. Sovereignty makes the state appear in history as a great violent individual facing other violent individuals. A universal state would be quite another thing: it would be essentially an educator-state directed toward liberty. But the changeover from this violent state to the educator-state is not yet in sight. States would have to wither away, at least qua sovereign and unconditionally violent, as mentioned above, in order to attain a stateless situation. At the moment quite the opposite is happening: we see the state multiplying its functions of organization, direction, planning. The process in which we are involved is rather that of the reinforcement of the State, and this reinforcement is taking place in the very epoch which should see the change from political expression to human community.

Of course, these views must be modified to some extent and, more important, must be set in their proper place. In many respects the State today is more a pretension than a reality, and its sovereignty is sometimes pure fiction. Already there is a practice of community of interest and interdependence which runs counter to the ways the State represents itself to itself or pretends to represent its importance to itself. All states are bound by conventions which are actual renunciations of sovereignty, even though these renunciations remain unacknowledged. This is why the allegation of sovereignty is so often contradicted by the facts. Even planning, which has the state as its support, is never purely national. The real power of decision is often other than one might think; this is why one must always be doing new analyses to discover where the real power of decision lies. This is the real question. Also one must take into account the discord, quite often camouflaged, between such sovereignty as is alleged or claimed and the effective exercise of the power of decision. Add to that the fact that changes of any kind modify this sovereignty: ideas circulate, models of organization and development are exchanged, and furthermore the very experience of international institutions exerts a certain educational force tending toward international life.

All this is true; nevertheless these various processes are dovetailed in a complex situation whose dominant note remains the principle of sovereignty. This is why we are presently incapable of proceeding to a complete transfer of sovereignty from the political entity "state" to that political entity of a new kind which a world sovereignty would require.

What gives the obstacle of the State its obduracy is the fact that it is so often doubled by the obstacle of the *nation*; the nation is that special community to which men have the consciousness of belonging, as to a geographical and historical unity of destiny. Until now it has always happened that the privileged form in which humanity has found the consciousness of its existence has been the nation. In the same way that we cannot actually conceive of a universal language with a literature, a history, etc., so humanity is conceivable only under the plural form of nations. Yet not only is the time of the nation not past, it appears to gather strength throughout the world, and that for reasons basic to this analysis.

First of all, the nation served as the instrument

for the conquest of identity: historical communities found the consciousness of what they were by means of the nation. One could say that the nation is for a historical community a form of representation of its own peculiar identity.

Decolonization reinforced this process, and we see why: colonization is a phenomenon not only of exploitation but also of the removal of personality; this is why decolonization must necessarily go through nationalism. The colonized must first of all recover their own proper identity.

Moreover the nation turns out to be valuable for withdrawal, as refuge, during the decline of ideologies. This can be seen today, when the ideological bonds of the communist block, and also those of the Atlantic block, are slackening; the nation is the value to which one withdraws while the ideological concentrations decompose. Hence also the prestige of Gaulism throughout the world: it represents in many respects this reconquest of national identity at the expense of an ideological identification which is the more or less coerced, more or less forced offspring of the cold war. In short, one could say that nationalism is the exacerbated and emotional expression of this consciousness that national worth is perennial in the face of the attempts at hegemony by the giant powers, camouflaged under the appearances of a collective hegemony.

But I think that there is another reason which makes the nation, or rather nationalism, difficult to overcome: the nation is also valuable as refuge and sustenance in the face of the threat of that leveling which industrial society represents. It is in terms of the nation that the struggle against anonymity, against being leveled out and absorbed by world industrial society, takes place. This industrial society, which I referred to above as a factor of human unification, also causes loss of identity; to a homogeneous science and a homogeneous technology stands opposed that plurality of life styles which are the nations. That is why there is every reason to think that the State and the nation, and in many cases the nation-state, will remain obdurate obstacles to the mondialization of politics.

Conjunctural obstacles

But we must give still more weight, no doubt, to conjunctural obstacles, to distortions which characterize the phenomena or development. The factors which we have reviewed are due to the structure of human experience, to the fact that it took shape in this form of nation-state. The obstacles of which we shall now speak are facts of conjuncture, that is, they result from the manner in which a certain number of developments occurred.

What can scarcely be overemphasized, as the Le Glay[2] conference confirms, is the seriousness of the present disparities in the world, first among which are *the disparities of an economic and social nature.* Inequality in the distribution of wealth and power is an enormous obstacle to the building of a world politics. As previously mentioned, this separation will continue to grow in the decades to come. On the one side are industrial power, technical capacity, financial resources, equipment in the sense of trained upper-level management; on the other side are dirt-cheap raw material, shortage of capital, shortage of trained personnel, the demographic obstacle. This growing disparity seriously affects the world order and makes the constitution of a true world politics impossible at the present time. Le Glay shows in another respect how the rise to industrial capacity of young nations differs from the comparable process which the presently industrialized countries underwent in the centuries just past. For the latter, industrialization was accomplished in a kind of void; in the case of the new nations the situation is quite otherwise. They arrive in a world already full, and the accomplished success of the first comers to well-being is an additional obstacle to the development of the late comers. This is why the notion of underdevelopment is so extraordinarily complex; there is not only a retarding, there is also a hindering.

Yet these disparities and underdevelopment are not only a real misfortune that affects certain historical communities; today these are forms of worldwide imbalance. Every analysis of underdevelopment must be taken from two different points of view; on the one hand, one must see what it means to the country under consideration, and on the other hand what it means, in terms of disorder, to the human community. In this way we ourselves are affected and concerned, insofar as our own development is an obstacle to the rapid development of others, an obstacle to the bringing about of a world economy. André Philip[3] showed only recently what underground conflicts of interest set the occidental masses in opposition to the masses of Africa, Asia and

143

South America; whether they want to or not, the first tend to defend their standard of living, their high wages, while at the same time they also tend to maintain the practice of low prices for the raw materials extracted from underdeveloped countries. This makes the interests of the working classes of the industrialized countries objectively at one with the global interests of the wealthy.

To this first distortion must be added another which is due to the *revolutionary consciousness in the world*. The fact that there exist today several revolutionary consciousnesses in the world is undoubtedly a factor, not only of diversity, but of distortion as well. I take into account here a recent analysis by Etienne Trocmé,[4] bearing on the three revolutionary attitudes currently in circulation: on one side the Chinese tendency toward permanent and uncompromising revolution; on the other, communism in the revisionist phase, trying to take into account the phenomena of the market-place and criteria of profit-making as intrinsic to their rigid planning, and finally the Third World revolutions, characterized by economic freedom delayed in favor of political freedom and by the distance between neo-capitalism, Chinese revolutionism, and the distributing and consolidating postures of accomplished revolutions. One could speak of this diversity of revolutionary models as a distorting phenomenon insofar as it contributes to the dismantling of the projects of world politics and more specifically of world economics. This competition is seen as intolerable disorder, mainly by the Third World, which finds itself confronted with models of development and with models of absolutely incompatible revolutions which present it with difficult choices and sometimes prevent it from producing a reformist or appropriately revolutionary model and force it to live off the borrowed revolutionary projects of others. Finally, to the economic disparities and to those disparities on the very level of revolutionary process are added the *political distortions* of an inherent character: we have been witnessing for several years the dissolution of a political directorate born of the war. The system of bilateral direction worked relatively well on at least one point, that of atomic dissuasion. The dissemination of atomic weapons created a new situation entirely: with the disintegration of the blacks, with the opening up of the atomic club to newcomers, we move from a game with two players to a game with *n* players, which creates a wholly fluid situation, less easily dealt with than was the previous bipolar system. Insofar as this new situation is less easily assessed in terms of prediction and control, it can be counted among the factors of disorder and among the conjunctural obstacles.

Perhaps we underestimate the *serious obstacle of racism*, the reduction of which to the phenomenon of the nation or of the State is problematic. The notion of race is scientifically illusory but psychologically powerful. Race is one of the ways in which humanity perceives itself; the moment that this notion has a psychological meaning, it is a cultural reality, a political reality. But we are far from having overcome this obstacle. We would have overcome it if we were capable of planning a completely interbred

145

humanity, of which we are rarely able fully to conceive; the situation of the American blacks, the South African and Rhodesian situations, remind us of it every day.

Must we add the obstacle represented by the notion of *continent*? It could be that in the coming decades the continent will be an important stage on the road to mondialization, but it could also be an obstacle, a period in which evolution could get stuck and where emotional phenomena of a new kind might take shape.

Such is the strange constellation of contemporary history, the combined play of planetary consciousness, structural obstacles and conjunctural obstacles.

I am willing to agree that this view is perhaps too antinomic; certainly we must take into account everything which modifies these contradictions and everything which opens gaps in them. In particular, I agree that we must not lock ourselves into too short a temporal perspective. We must learn to think in terms of *long periods of time.* The winning of rationality and the modern State has been long and slow; the placing and the empowering of a practice regulated by the global interest of humanity will likewise no doubt require decades, perhaps centuries. But this thinking in terms of long periods of time has not yet trickled down to the level of public opinion and individual consciousness. For instance, long-term consideration of all the gropings toward a world economy would be needed; all the endless conferences on disarmament, on the price of raw materials, on investments, on aid and co-operation agreements are indeed a manifestation of the slowness of history in bringing about the change from the nation-state to a world government of the global interests of mankind. In the same way one must give long-term consideration to the transformation of socialist revolutions, the accommodation of capitalism to its opposite, the trials and errors directed toward the achievement of composite forms between socialism and communism which are in process nearly everywhere throughout the world. In these long, slow developments, peaceful coexistence, co-operation between different social systems, and, perhaps, the appearance of certain convergences, or even better, of certain amalgamations, come into play. On the other hand, apart from the fact that these openings and these ongoing experiments must be taken into account, one may no longer underestimate the importance of conflicts as evolutionary factors; our history is conspicuous for the quest for convergences, but also by the proliferation of conflicts. One must be Marxist on this point: conflicts are also a means of grasping consciousness and of the advance of history. Thus we should not restrict ourselves to a static view of obstacles and difficulties; instead we should arrive at a dynamic vision of the situation. In such a way we open up a field of action.

PART TWO

A COMPLEX TASK . . .

It seems today that Christian action in the world depends upon a proper relation between three factors: first, the formulation of a new preaching to the world; secondly, the church's theological readjustment of itself and of its relationship to the world; thirdly, a capacity for the involvement of its members in lay action. Upon the balance of these three factors depends the health of the church's presence in the world. One could speak in this sense of the "tripod" of the church's presence in the world.

Toward a preaching to the world

We must begin with the theme of the new preaching to the world, for theology is never first; it is always a second-degree reflection which presupposes the practice of precisely that preaching and that involvement.

I distinguish here *preaching to the faithful* from *preaching to the world.*

Preaching to the faithful has an exact function: that of preserving the nucleus of the confessional community which collectively carries this preaching to the world. The finality of the preaching to the faithful is that there was such a confessional community which was the collective bearer of this preaching to the world. For another reason the preaching to the faithful can be only a part of the preaching: as analysis of the international situation shows us, historical Christianity is a sociological reality of an increasingly minority status. Consequently, if the church has a message for the world and about the political problems of the world, this message must be expressed in some way that is not concerned with the confessional community. Whence the necessity for a preaching to all men. And this message will have even more scope and weight as

148

the procedure toward the direct dismantling of confessional institutions continues in another respect and is carried out: confessional trade union, confessional party, etc. What is perhaps the greatest obstacle to this preaching to the world is the persistence of a kind of social Catholicism (or even Protestantism) which is a product of the 19th century, a clericalism of the left which merely replaces the clericalism of the right. The new type of witnessing which will appear must be completely dissociated from any institutional aspect. It must be the harbinger or a message without power of any kind that addresses politics in order to exhort and warn. In this respect Paul VI's speech to the UN seems to me quite exemplary; not that all that he said was good, but that the act itself was good, in the right place and fully significant.

In today's world one must bring about a new articulation of the spiritual and the political and, through this articulation, must stress the process of the mondialization of problems, solutions and politics itself. We are in effect searching for a new equilibrium between the spiritual and the political, which is not the balance between two powers, as the Middle Ages conceived it, but one between a witnessing and the lay power of men. For this to come about, both the spiritual and the political must find their proper aims.

I connect this kind of reflection to a type of analysis I have often done, here and elsewhere, concerning the articulation of two moral principles, that of personal conviction which represents the fundamental aims of man, and that of responsibility

149

and force which concerns the exercise of public power.

This preaching touches both the political and the social levels. First at the political level: *politics* is healthy, insofar as this preaching and this principle of conviction protects it from its demons, enables it to find its proper place, allows it to "de-absolutize" itself, and protects it from becoming in its turn a new religion, a lay religion; it is the task of this preaching to place it and keep it in its place. Paul VI used the right word when he introduced himself as an "expert in humanity." Indeed it is in this that spiritual power consists: to preserve the aim of humanity, to denounce courageously the obstacles to the unity of the human species, to expose publicly the interplay of distortions, to attack the good conscience of the wealthy, to denounce nationalism and the cult of the State, and consequently to take a stand with the greatest clarity on the limitation of sovereignty, and to show in the international institutions centered around the UN the only chance presently offered to men to move on beyond the stage of the nations. As we see, it is not at all a matter of blessing the UN but rather of giving it the only kind of consecration which is appropriate to it, namely, the supreme motivation which consists in the aim of man as such.

It is also inevitable that this preaching must take a stand on *socio-economic* planning. In the face of the growing gap between rich and poor, it must urge political systems to find economic forms of welfare. André Philip says in another connection that the redistribution of monetary means and the improvement of living standards of the "underde-veloped" runs directly counter to the short-term interests of *all* social groups in the industrialized countries. We cannot practice a politics based on short-term interest; this short-term interest, in-cluding that of the working classes of the indus-trialized nations, moves in the direction of the defense of high standards of living and consequently coincides with the short-term interests of the ruling classes. This is why only that ethical motivation which is the consciousness of belonging to humanity as such can reinforce the long-term human interest in working out a world-wide economy of needs. One should mention here what Paul VI said about political structure: in international institutions the people are not equal, but they make themselves equal. It is this will to become "equal" in the political structure and in the socio-economic structure which must be sustained and motivated by this preaching of justice and equality.

Toward a theological task

I place as second the church's theological read-justment of itself. This is its place relative to the preaching to the world.

What the theologian should rediscover here is that true Christian universalism which is a universalism of "intention" completely distinct from the uni-versalist "pretension" of the Christianity of the Constantinian Age. Only to the extent that this Chris-tianity dies does that universalism become meaningful.

The struggle of the universalist *intention* against the universalist *pretension* has roots going back to

151

the Bible. There we find its inverse image in the struggle between two particularisms, a particularism of intention and a particularism of pretension. In other words, within the theological frame of reference the true sense of Israel's Calling has been won with difficulty from the most extraordinary particularism in history. For example in the Book of Joshua, which is the most striking in this respect, there is an interpretation of the destiny of the people of Israel in which the Alliance is essentially conceived as a non-mergence with others, as a non-alliance, in a fanatical particularism, that is to say, theologically fanatical. The account of the wars of Joshua demonstrates this most strikingly. Even though current historical reconstruction inclines us to the view that the settling in Canaan did not have the character of an extermination as described in the Bible, the very fact that the Israelites mythologized their own infiltration as a war of extermination is theologically significant. It was necessary that this particularism be turned against itself as a particularism of another kind so that Israel's significance among nations might appear in its true light: the election of Israel is the singular election of a people of whom humanity as a whole is the recipient and beneficiary. "In thee all nations will be blessed (will bless themselves)."[5] Here we have a form of the election of the Church which is for humanity as a whole: in thee all nations bless themselves. The election only makes sense as pertaining to this kind of appropriation by all people, individually and collectively, of the concrete significance of the benediction of Israel. It is noteworthy that this *particularism qua*

152

universalist calling was authentic only insofar as it did not achieve political success: Israel never clarified its own political significance, varying between monarchy, the power of the priests and the power of the law. It is to the extent that this "universalist particularism" (if one might venture such a paradox) remained authentic that Israel was capable of representing humanity to itself as a totality and, beyond humanity, all creation as a divine work. I am thinking here of the attempted genealogy in Genesis, which testifies to a first attempt at a theology of history, and to that pagan theology which appears now and again: "Cyrus, my servant. . . "[6] And finally I am thinking of that great eschatology of the Last Supper and of the reconciliation of all things on the day of judgment.[7]

It is this *universalism of intention* which in this context is recovered, in the figure of *Christ*; I am thinking of the interpretation, more or less mythological but powerfully symbolic, of the drama of the Cross, understood not as a local event, but as a cosmic drama relating to man, all men. Man is conceived, in extension and in depth, as a collected unity faced with the drama of the Cross. Here too, one must cry: "In thee all nations will bless themselves."[8] What is meant by this enormous emphasis on a particular event, transposed into a universal significance, is man complete, man indivisible, beyond all political particularism. St. Paul was the first to have conceived of and meditated on this kind of "mondialization" of the Cross as he projected it beyond human differences: "There is neither Jew nor Greek, there is neither slave nor free."[9]

From this mondialization of the Cross comes a kind of negativism applied to the present differences of the socio-economic and political order.

But this theological reflection is inseparable from the preaching to all men. Cut off from the latter, it turns to abstract theology, which is to say mythology. If this reflection ceases to be interpreted into an action which promotes humanity as a whole, if I do nothing to make humanity become a whole, the utopia of total humanity becomes a myth.

Consequently the preaching to man, to universal man, is nothing; it is even a lie and a deception if the Church does not show, by concrete signs, how it has overcome differences of nation, differences of economic and social levels, differences resulting from the cold war. And the combination of forces of the ecumenical movement and the Catholic Church would not be sufficient for these concrete signs to exist. This very combination can be quite ambiguous. Here even Mario Miegge[10] warned against a trap into which the ecumenical movement might always fall; it is quite possible that Christians could effect a reconciliation among themselves and with the other religious men in the world to form a barrier against atheistic communism. This coalition of the established religions against atheism and communism would be entirely contrary to the concrete sign for which men are waiting. It would be one more particularist coalition, extending the theology of the wars of Joshua rather than that of the congregation of Israel among the nations. The signs are always ambiguous, and that the sign of ecumenism be inscribed in the line of the universalism of intention and not in that of the universalism of pretension depends upon the vigilance of all, and upon ourselves.

A word addressed and an action undertaken[11]

This is why the theological task is interdependent, on the one hand, with a preaching to all men, on the other with the commitment of Christians, individually or collectively, to "mondialist" or "mondializing" actions. I have purposely placed the theological task between the preaching and the commitment as a reflexive articulation between these two poles: a word addressed and an action undertaken.

I specifically said the commitment of Christians, for the commitment of the Church as such which is its preaching, must be clearly distinguished from the commitment of Christians which is under the law of merger with other men. Only insofar as there is a specific preaching and a collective commitment is there also a theology.

It seems to me that we are faced with three kinds of commitments. To begin with there are those commitments which are of a traditional style but which cannot, simply for that reason, be impugned: this is *protest action* at the level of leaflets, declarations, proposals. I give as example participation in campaigns against the French atomic bomb, against the spread of atomic weapons on a world-wide level, and for the extending of the Moscow accords to include the outlawing of underground explosions and destruction of stockpiles and delivery systems. All this is necessary and must be intensified. There would be quite a serious danger in eliminating this type of intervention; it is bound up with the ideological struggle which is the fight at the level of those overriding principles and global conceptions which dominate the technological problems of international (political or social) life, and the recent period of ideological excess has been followed by a disturbing ideological ebb. I agree that during the past few decades politics has been quite often perverted by an overindulgence in empty declarations and overly general protests; this type of protest often needs to be more rigorously and precisely made to fit the ever more technical nature of the problems. In any movement of this kind, the delicate question arises as to the direct interaction of the militants and the specialists. There is a general tendency of political and economic action today to place upon the specialists the responsibility for decisions which are in reality political rather than technical in nature. The technocracy, so-called, is not the invention of the technocrats but the result of the political resignation of the militants. Thus the protest action question itself is only the most widespread aspect of Christian commitment. We must find the proper balance between misuse of phraseology and ideological combat at the level of significant alternatives and global conceptions of society.

On the other hand there is an action which presupposes the concrete practice of *encounter situations*. I am not speaking here of the encounter of man with man, which is more an ethical than a political problem. When I speak of encounter situations I mean here collective situations and organized encounters: the problem of the migrants, the problem of technological co-operation, the problem of the international education of the young gives us our prime examples. These are experienced situations of encounter in the sense that the structures which we attack express themselves immediately in the lot which today is destined to fall to a substantial number of men: the problem of migration is that of the arrival of underdevelopment at our city gates. What we encounter in our shanty-towns is the under-developed world projected into the very heart of industrialized countries. The problem of co-opera-tion,[12] by contrast, is that of an encounter in the opposite direction between technicians coming from the developed countries and the authorities of countries still on the road to development.

This encounter is a commitment of a very sig-nificant kind: the situations in which it places certain men may not merely aid them, they may also produce conflict. The danger is twofold: to prolong the sly forms of paternalism under the guise of technological co-operation, which is to say neo-colonialism, or to become accustomed, through flattery, to compromise with political groups which are not always motivated by the best interests of their people. It is the same with international educa-tion of the young: the encounters of young workers or students breach the wall of nationalism. Through these encounters ideas and experiences circulate as prejudices fall, but there is also the danger that these encounters could turn toward folklore or toward fraternization without any impact on those structures which have extraordinary power of resistance to change (as has been shown elsewhere).

This practice of experiencing situations of encounter still remains the way in which that can be lived which, at the theological level, can only be thought: St. Paul's dictum that there is neither Jew nor Greek, there is neither slave nor free.

The third action-group is our entry into the level of *international institutions*, such as the FAO,[13] OMS,[14] UNESCO, etc. I know that there are complaints that these international organizations lack the presence and commitment of dedicated men, of men of faith in every sense of the word, at the level of conception, of planning, of execution. Nevertheless it is there that we can find an opportunity for encounter at a level on which men are thoroughly mixed and mingled; there are few places where one can stand at the edge of so extraordinarily varied a human sampling; it is there also that mass action and specialist action are found together. Finally, it is there that ideological combat is carried out through a work of genuine co-operation.

The range is thus wide open, extending from ideological combat to the practice of international institutions and passing through the experienced situations of encounter between the developed and the underdeveloped.

NOTES

1. From *mondial*, meaning "world-wide" or "one-world," Ricoeur has coined the terms *mondialism, mondialist, mondializing,* and *mondialization,* for the theory, the promoter, the promoting, and the realizing of the world state. Where translation into standard English is excessively cumbersome, Ricoeur's neologisms have been anglicized. *Tr.*

2. The LeGlay Conference was sponsored by *Le Christianisme Social* and was held in one of the few Protestant areas of France. *Ed.*

From Nation to Humanity: Task of Christians

3. President of the Socialist Movement for the United States of Europe, member of the Law Faculty, University of Paris, and author of *Christianity and Socialism*, and *Toward a Humanistic Socialism*.

4. Professor of New Testament at the University of Strasbourg, and editor of *Le Christianisme social* and *Revue d'histoire et de philosophie religieuse*.

5. Genesis 22:18; 26:4; cf. Acts 3:25. *Ed.*

6. Isaiah 45:1. *Ed.*

7. Matthew 26:28; Mark 14:24. *Ed.*

8. *See* Acts 3:25. *Ed.*

9. Galatians 3:28. *Ed.*

10. Professor of Pedagogy, University of Urbino, and author of "Communism and the Church," and "Catholic Ecumenism" in *Protestantismo* (Italy).

11. *Engagée*. With *engagement*, these two terms are variously translated "involvement," "undertaking," "commitment," and "interaction" as the context requires. *Tr.*

12. Refers to the French policy of aid to former colonies. *Ed.*

13. Food and Agricultural Organization. *Ed.*

14. Organization for the Maintenance of Supplies. *Ed.*

8

THE PROJECT OF A SOCIAL ETHIC

THE QUESTION

IN A CHRISTIAN CONTEXT THE PROBLEM OF A SOCIAL ethic is frequently represented as the construction of a coherent doctrine intended, on the one hand, to fill the void between Christian preaching and, on the other hand, judgment and decisions of a technical nature concerning the administration of society considered mainly from the angle of industrial society. In order to fill in this intermediary function, a social ethic should include three steps or three levels:

The social ethics of the Bible

Under this heading are classified the "social teachings" derived from the prophets and from the preaching of Jesus and the apostles. Biblical theology was burdened with disengaging from exegesis a coherent, timely system of valid precepts.

Translated by David Stewart

The Project of a Social Ethic

The social doctrine of the church

By that one can mean the successive systems constituted in the Middle Ages, in the period of the Reformation, or in modern times—in view of the amalgamation of prior principles with major concepts of social philosophy. Hence the concepts of distributive and commutative justice and the city or human community are borrowed from Aristotle and the Stoics. Recovered from the Middle Ages are the different notions of natural and social rights, which were followed even to the time of Rousseau. The modern notion of contract was borrowed from the philosophers of the eighteenth century. And finally, Hegel furnished all contemporaries with "historical" concepts (alienation, dialectic, rationality and facticity, etc.). What we have thus called the social doctrine of the church has represented, on the Catholic side, a continually deceptive attempt to recapture medieval concepts in order to renew them with modern concepts of varied origins. On the Protestant side one has worked most often on the basis of concepts often borrowed from the Reformation, from Kantianism and neo-Kantianism, and from the Hegelian and post-Hegelian phase of social philosophy. Liberal theologies have created some very significant amalgams from these diverse concepts even up to our own time.

The confrontation of global systems

This third level of social ethics represents an effort of criteriology, i.e., of coherent discrimination at the level of systems: socialism, capitalism, liberalism, collectivism. It is with this third stage

161

that the title "social ethics" is indeed often associated, blocking by this judgment the three stages that we want to examine. Indeed, this discrimination has frequently consisted in a skill of "lesser evil"; it expresses in fact the skill of the moralist, that is to say, an exercise of practical judgment closest to reality and social practice but on the level of the ideology of a system. Beyond that begins the judgment of circumstance in terms of concrete situations and particular obligations.

For many of our contemporaries, it is still this schema which represents the "social ethic" of Christianity, i.e., to know a document of thought, of judgment, and of action in which the three points of view that we want to examine could be connected. If the operation were possible, it would not be the solution for the continuity between Christian preaching and politico-social engagement, the blending opened up on the theological, philosophical and ideological levels.

The preliminary question which it is necessary for us to pose is this: Is our task today to ameliorate, to rejuvenate, to see how to make this kind of doctrine more coherent? Or indeed, is it necessary to renounce it entirely?

To tell the truth, whether this project blows to bits does not depend on us.

A better exegesis and a better biblical theology has almost made impossible the search for universal principles based on scripture. Biblical criticism invites us rather to place in their own context and to understand according to their own intention such notions as the kingdom of God, justice, law, covenant, etc. It is possible to disengage principles and eternal values, but it has become more and more difficult— indeed impossible—to combine the kerygmatic pro- clamation with the concepts of political and social philosophy.

The metaphysics which could support this philosophi- cal-theological discourse have mostly collapsed, or else they have become problematic themselves and only survive in the mood of an open question. It is not possible to grasp social ethics at the stage one could call the crisis of metaphysics and of the pro- cess of destruction and reconstruction in which it henceforth is to be engaged.

The ideologies which frequently supplied an inter- mediate step are in crisis themselves. We are in a phase of ideological ebb on all fronts. One can understand why; ideology is frequently the refuge of hollow phrases, alibis, and falsehoods. But even more serious, global society less and less takes refuge in remote and idealistic intentions but re- solves its problems more and more on the basis of present technology. Effective intervention in in- dustrial society has essentially become the affair of specialists, who reason less from great principles as on the basis of a reasonable empiricism. The global systems inherited from the ideological period —capitalism, socialism—are treated as boundaries, given facts, in the context of which communities have the task of living and surviving. The problem is set in place by regulative mechanisms permitting these systems to function empirically in a more coherent fashion and thus shelters each from internal crises and from a rupture exerted from without by a rival system.

The great project of a systematic and coherent social ethic is thus torn to pieces. Biblical theology is rejected on the side of exegesis and feels itself more and more estranged from the working-out of everlasting principles. It is rather concerned with disengaging from the Bible the meaning of the concrete behavior of men and the value of the testimony and the sign which is attached to the events and institutions of the biblical past. On the other extreme we have an increasingly neutral technique which is more and more distrustful regarding principles, values, and ideas. The decline of ideologies widens the gap a little more between biblical "signs" and regulative "techniques" applicable to economic and social mechanisms.

Such is the junction which dominates our present research. What is to be done in this situation? In my judgment we are no longer—or not yet—in the age of great syntheses. A total and coherent structure will today be a deception. The only way open today is that of a method of approximation and convergence. On the one hand, it is necessary to look in social reality for the discontinuous, unstable, and varying points of insertion for Christian preaching. On the other hand, it is necessary to start from the work of specialists bearing on such well determined points as work, business undertakings, information, and so forth, and not to look for their insertion in a system—in a whole—but to disengage their most concrete and historic affinities with biblical teaching. In short it is necessary *to place the biblical concrete in direct contact with the social exact.*

LOCATING POINTS OF INSERTION

For my part I will start with the two extreme points opposed where the intention of action is the clearest.

At one extreme it seems to me that one can affirm that today humanity is the unique subject of history. Scripture speaks of man as one generic being; creation, the fall, redemption concern man. "You have been created barely inferior to a god. . . ."[1] (it should not be forgotten that scripture speaks thus of nations and peoples and individuals that it names and calls; more about that later). But we are the first epoch that can give content and meaning to this project. The destiny of humanity as a unique subject is the figure which stands out in all our debates on hunger in the world, on the atomic menace, decolonization, the quest for a world order and, perhaps more than anything, what Perroux[2] calls the generalized economy. But this unity of humanity cannot be achieved all by itself. It cannot function as a cybernetic machine which corrects and repairs itself. This grand design is pursued through what I have called the pathology of this generic being. We know the signs; in the very epoch where we reflect on humanity, the rich become always richer and the poor always poorer. Great powers intend to regulate the destiny of the world by sharing of influence. Diverse nationalisms are consolidated and enflamed. The receding ideologies break economic rationality to pieces on the level of the great international exchanges. The world economy of needs is restrained by the rivalries and politics of prestige. Therefore I think that our action and social thought ought to be polarized by the will to make prevail the needs of humanity taken as a whole. Such is the unifying value with regard to all our particular projects.

At the other extreme I see another task: to personalize to the maximum the relations which become abstract, anonymous, and inhuman in industrial society. It is necessary, then, to grasp social ethics by another end. What obtains here are concrete actions on the part of small, effective groups. The struggle against dehumanization in the great urban sprawls, in psychiatric hospitals, homes for the elderly, etc. . . furnish us with the model of what one could call a personalistic action. The intention of this action, like the preceding, constitutes a utopia, i.e., that each man should be entirely fulfilled. I recapture willingly the word of Spinoza: "The more we know singular things, the more we know God." For my part, a social ethic cannot spring from a system but from a paradox. It aims at two opposed things: human totality and human singularity. I want both. Their full and non-contradictory realization will be the kingdom of God. From that social ethics receives its dual motivation—communal and personalistic.

Starting from this initial polarity, how can one find his bearings? What is there between the individual person and humanity taken as a whole? The question is strange, since it is precisely everything social that extends between these two poles.

I think that one's judgment should not be cloudy at the ideological level.

The exercising of critical judgment at the level of global social systems (capitalism, socialism, etc.) is legitimate on the condition that one never separates the ideology which they appeal to and the effective action concerning real relations between real men. Therefore it matters less to perceive the abstract right of property than real power and its exercise by real groups. Moreover, it is always necessary for us to compare what is comparable and not, for example, to compare the real form of one system with the ideal form of another. I think that it would be necessary to begin all our analyses of socialism again in order to locate well the level of our judgment. I should think that the systems ought to be appreciated most concretely in their function of the double intention toward humanity as a whole and towards the single person.

How is one now as a "social Christian" to approach the small unities and means, such as business, the industrial branch, the economic plan, the common market, and so forth? I well know that this is essential to the social problem, but it is also the most difficult. I principally see these questions: How far do the technical and automatic aspects of socio-economic judgments exclude ethical judgment? What effect can ethical judgment have? When we formulate them, to what are we addressing them, which is to say, who can receive and apply them? The question of the point of insertion is posed here in a grave fashion: on what are they brought to bear? We risk

167

either concentrating on the automatisms and their neutrality with regard to every ethical judgment or, on the contrary, ignoring in moralistic naïveté the determinisms on which we can act. It seems to me that the question is concentrated on the notion of the center of decision. It is at the point where the decision is made that ethical considerations can be applied. Thus the choice of the planner is a wager on a conception of man, his needs, and his destiny.

It is necessary to see how far one can lead a preliminary reflection on the polarity expressed before, i.e., intended toward humanity as a whole and intended toward the single person. To what point are we able to draw out a criterion concerning it? For example, are we to say that the good is both that which increases communication and that which multiplies responsibilities? At the level of means, the latter will be the expression of two projects which we have distinguished from the two extremities of human action. Has it not been said in the past that riches are poverty because they break up community, because they enslave, and because they isolate? Since the conditions of an ethical judgment in social matters will be to search, not at the technical level, but for motivations, what man is willing to do it? What can man do effectively? It is with such questions that we can be oriented in a critical manner in the reform of business, economic planning, European unification, etc. Thus this question concerns the man who is willing and able to cause more attention to be directed to the effective relations between men rather than to systems simply alleged or pretended.

THE CONVERGING INVESTIGATIONS

Instead of improving a sham doctrine debatable in principle and disputed in reality, we rather have to co-ordinate formerly determined works expressing a particular competence in a limited field, even if they do not allow us to distinguish a whole plan.

Biblical Theology

First I see a relatively closed but well-expressed harmony in contemporary Catholic and Protestant biblical theology. What is most valuable for us in this domain is not, paradoxically, the abstract reflection on the social ethics of the prophets, the Sermon on the Mount, or the letters of Paul. In the Bible there are not principles and ideals in the sense of a theoretical ethics but imprecations, stories, parables, exhortations, promises and praises which must be understood according to their own meaning and in their historic context. What is finally most instructive for action are the most concrete and specific studies on the kingdom, the new man, the world, sin, law, the life according to the flesh, and the life according to the Spirit. We are sure to find our good there because the Bible ignores the individual, in the sense of the modern consciousness, and addresses itself to the man who is always called upon as a person situated in a concrete community. This is because there is not any distinction in scripture between private ethics and social ethics that we are taught in all concrete situations. It will therefore be fruitless to search in scripture for divine principles which allow us to deduce from them other profane principles. The articulation to look for is of another order: at the level of motivation, of exemplification and analogy, which is another thing than abstract deduction.

A second group of specific studies concerns the investigations respecting *man in industrial society*. I think that this group of studies is nearest the preceding, although it is not at all possible to be deduced from it. I see at least four sub-groups.

Workingman

It is here that the best work has been done or is in process. It is in fact a question of a cluster of investigations, themselves most discontinuous and speaking from multiple points of view, but constituting a *convergent group*. Speaking from the biblical and patristic pole, one investigates the significance of human work. Speaking from the technological pole, one studies the evolution of work in industrial societies, the effects of mechanization and its crumbling, its relation to wage earners, business management, and leisure. The concept of the civilization of work has served as a "covering" for well-executed studies which explore the connections between theology, ethics, sociology, and technology. The elements of judgment are able to give rise to the confluence of these investigations. I think that it has already disengaged certain criteria concerning the conditions in which work remains meaningful.

The Project of a Social Ethic

In particular, it has disengaged itself from the impression that the questions of meaning and meaninglessness are today as important as those of justice and equality. But here again it is not necessary to start with the abstract but with the biblical and human concrete.

The investigation of human needs

Man no longer pursues what he makes but what he desires. It is from this bias that the problems of finality are fruitfully approached. Here also the most concrete studies are those which start with non-satisfied needs in the world (hunger in the world, etc.), taking consciousness of needs in the particular circumstances of industrial society. This study is always concrete because, depending on systems of appropriation, social stimuli (advertising), or traditional values, human need does not have the same meaning. Thus an expanding society does not incite in the same manner as a stable society, etc. These concrete investigations can be coupled with the most theoretical investigations into the hierarchy among vital needs, personal needs, cultural needs, and spiritual needs. In this second cluster of convergence the examination of the finality of modern society ought to be included and taken into account. What do the well-being and autonomy of persons aim at? And what does enjoyment and satisfaction mean nowadays? What is the implicit idea of happiness? Do the world governments have the same goal? And even more radically, does industrial society have this goal, or indeed is it

171

enslaved to means without ends? Here one encounters not only the problem of values—justice, liberty— but meaning or the absence of meaning. Modern man is perhaps more deprived of meaning than of justice.

These studies allow the unfortunate attempts to establish the catalogs of human rights (liberty, equality, etc.) to be pulled from the rut. These catalogs are an abstract projection at a given moment of attained satisfactions and immediate demands. It is certainly not our task to improve this catalog.

Property and socialization

A third sub-group will be pretty well placed under the heading (borrowed from *Economie et humanisme*[3]) "Property and Socialization." The industrial era has imposed profound modifications on the order of individual property delineated at the dawn of the nineteenth century. Production agreements have taken on collective dimensions, conferring on their holders an exorbitant economic power. The system of private appropriation is profoundly altered in all its aspects by the universal phenomenon of socialization. What will be the consequence for men? Here, also, the only way of proceeding is to group together reflections on such principles as the right of every man to use material goods for his own preservation, or the primacy of the community over the interests of individuals, groups, etc.; and on the other hand, the study of the evolution of legal systems in the world; and finally, concrete investigations concerning the exercise of power, pressure groups, business groups, organizers, etc.

172

The Project of a Social Ethic

Technics and technology

There is a particular problem peculiar to technics because we are the first historic society in which technics is the dominant phenomenon. It is this dominant character which calls for a reflection of which we today still do not see the coherent features. It is necessary here again to proceed by convergence: on the one hand a reflection on the idea of the uniformity of a society which thinks of itself as exploiting nature and dominating life and psychism; on the other hand a concrete study bearing on the transformation of human work, industrialization, leisure, mass culture, etc.

A third group of investigations is constituted by the *critique of global social systems*: capitalism and socialism. I place this at the third level in order to underscore well that social ethics is not limited to a criteriology of systems (socialism is better than capitalism because . . .). This critique does not itself constitute a single problem but a cluster of problems. There is, on the one hand, the ideology of the systems; that is, the manner in which they are represented theoretically in the thought of their founders, apologists, and theoreticians. On the other hand, there are the practical aspects of systems, which are the effective social relations of a capitalistic or socialistic regime. Any judgment concerning systems ought to take account of this dialectic of theory and practice. It ought to engage in considerations concerning the person and the community with particular structures and ideologies. Abstract discussions concerning the

173

right of property, distributive justice, profit, regulation by needs or by services, ought not to be separated
from their role in determined situations. Monographs
concerning particular regimes ought always to correct treatises on doctrines.

Today a sub-group of problems seems to be detached from the preceding: what is the true role of
the global social system in industrial societies? Is
there a problem of industrial society as such (the
problem of Raymond Aron)? At what level does this
society create a convergence greater than the
divergence of systems? Can these convergences be
attributed to the effects of the mutual adjustment
of one system on the others or on the effects of
syncretism, i.e., a dose of liberalism being injected
into collectivism and modern collectivism absorbing
a growing quantity of socialization? Or indeed are
these convergences the effect of industrialization
as such? These questions, as is obvious, rejoin the
earlier reflections on technics.

A fourth group of investigations—the most scattered yet the most important for daily action—concern the *unities of production* and is centered on
business. It is there that ethical judgment is the
most difficult to exercise. This will be a particular
task of our later investigations, which will ask what
is the point of application for ethical reflection.
What does the reform of business mean? How can
the human prevail in it? And what is human in business?

I think, therefore, the social ethics defines a
level of judgment much more than a system constituted or to be constituted. This is the field of a

varied, multidimensional, discontinuous reflection. The convergence of concrete studies is always better than the false logic of systems.

NOTES

1.   Ricoeur is here paraphrasing Psalm 8:5. *Ed.*
2.   Francoise Perroux, noted French economist and author of *La Coexistence pacifique*, 2 vols. (1958); *Ećonomie et société* (1960); *L'Ećonomie du xxᵉ siécle* (1961); *L'Ećonomie des jeunes nations* (1962); and *Industrie et création collective* (1964). *Ed.*
3.   A. Rubin, *Economie et humanisme: Éxpose analytique* (St. Paul: Friburg, 1958). *Ed.*

9

Urbanization and Secularization

THE PURPOSE OF THIS ACCOUNT IS TWOFOLD: (A) TO explore the relations between the phenomenon of urbanization taken at its furthest point of development and the cultural phenomenon of secularization; (b) to explore the tasks presented today to a theology of culture and, more generally, to the church's preaching in the city, in an age of secularization.

The first of these two projects is already quite sizable. It directly involves two very important sociological facts, relating to different methods: on the one hand, urban sociology which is itself part of the sociology of advanced industrial societies, and on the other hand, the sociology of culture.[1]

THE CITY

In beginning with the phenomenon of urbanization, I wish to consider a certain number of features

Translated by Hoke Robinson

chosen as possibilities offered to man by the large city in order eventually to confront them with the phenomenon of secularization.

Multiplication, Abstraction, and Elongation of Relations and Interchanges. The phenomenon "city" would be missed if its quantitative aspect alone were taken into account; it is not entirely, nor even partially, defined by characterizing it as a human aggregate in a concentrated space. The city is first of all a fact of communication similar to an enormous exchange or a giant name-board. It institutes among men a dense ramified network of interhuman relations, which grow not only more numerous but also longer, more varied, more specialized, and more abstract. To man, this means ever more numerous occasions both for encounter and for choice. The phenomenon could be expressed in terms of information: a man is subjected by the city to a flood of signals and is forced to decode these messages which widen simultaneously his field of information and his field of decision. Together with Harvey Cox, I am interested in what is normally presented as an ill of modern civilization: the anonymity of human relations. This must be described first of all in neutral terms as a new division between the private and the public, and even more fundamentally, as a defense reaction or even an immunization against the innumerable outside intrusions which result from a multiplicity of contacts. In order to initiate or protect those personal relations which are freely chosen and prized, one has no choice but to neutralize most social interchanges; the *socius* becomes tolerable only insofar as a large number of relations remains fragmentary. Thus this depersonalization of most of our relations has a positive aspect to the extent that it preserves a domain of authentic encounters. This at least means that not all social relations can be transcribed into the language of "I" and "thou."

Accelerated Mobility (geographic, residential, professional, social, psychological, and so forth). The city may be described as an environment of internal migration. This phenomenon is bound up with the preceding one since it is this migration which inaugurates the relations and contacts noted before. But mobility adds a new feature: for most people, the place of residence and the place of work are widely separated. This geographical distance symbolizes a psychological distance; the different roles are disparate and disjointed. The changing of roles takes the form of a voyage, sometimes of a dislocation, always of an "estrangement." This mobility represents an unavoidable ordeal for modern man. It forces him to change socially, and sometimes professionally; it requires a great deal of flexibility in adjustment and confrontation. While lowering the thresholds of acceptance and tolerance, it makes encounters between rival convictions more difficult, causing them to oscillate between aggressiveness and indifference. Moreover, accelerated mobility is not felt in the same way by all social groups. For the underprivileged, this uprooting is the hard road of adaptation to the modern world, as all migrants well know; if mobility is ultimately liberating for them, it is at the price of considerable suffering. For the privileged, mobility often takes the form of trip and vacation; its cultural effects are largely beneficial in spite of the nomadism and deracination which accompanies them.

Concentrated Organization. The geographical concentration previously mentioned is only the superficial and quantitative aspect of a much more important functional phenomenon which has its source in the modern method of organizing work. The "metropolis" is a "technopolis." It is dominated by the bureaucratic model of division and organization of labor. The city is that place where the conversion of the primary sector into the secondary (former peasants and artisans becoming city dwellers) and the rapid growth of areas of responsibility (trade and distribution, administration and social relations, education and laws, etc.) is physically felt. The urban concentration of the bureaucratic management of industry, banking systems, the machinery of distribution, of exchange and retail, demonstrates to all the reign of the organization man. Around this technological core is distributed the quite diverse system of public education, sanitation, recreation, the legal institutions, etc. All of that makes the city the logistical apparatus of social roles.

The City's Self-image. The collective picture men hold of their city is a part of the "city-phenomenon" which is as important as the reality of the situation. There is always an image of the city. Visualize the mythical images of the "civitas"; the visible face of a heavenly patron (Babylon, Jerusalem, actually all of the *civitates dei*); visualize also the Greek identification of the city and the political unit (*polis*).

179

But we have another and more modern image for ourselves, a perception of the city which makes it the major witness to human energy: the city is the inverse of the earth, product of nature; the city is the complete artifact, the realized human project. This sign of man's power is at the same time a sign of a force essentially directed toward the future. The city is always building, looking to its own future. The city is where man perceives change as a human project, the place where man perceives his proper "modernity."

Is this to say that the city has only positive aspects? I have described it in neutral terms as a new way humans can relate to one another. This opportunity, this chance is experienced by turns as liberation and as constraint; liberation from the constraints of town and village, constraint of a new sort. I do not intend to deny the *pathology* of the city which is inextricably mixed with the search for a new balance in its movement. It is precisely because this pathology is felt to be unbearable today that there is such a thing as "urbanism." Urbanism is the reply to urban pathology. Urbanism means that the city cannot continue to grow according to its natural movement; its movement must be dominated, controlled, directed. Not only is there a pathology of the city, but this pathology is the awesome expression of the pathology of global society; it plays the role of the abscess, drawing corruption and draining it with respect to diffused sociological sickness.

Each of the four features around which we have arranged our description presents its own pathology.

Communication? We feel it as an excess of signals, a flood of information which exhausts, in both the physical and psychical senses of the word, our capacity to integrate and discriminate. The congestion of our cities is the symbol of a general pathological feature, the swelling and saturation of relations which no longer link up. We also know that anonymity is not only a way of immunizing ourselves against excess signals and signs but a subtle destruction of private life itself.

Mobility? It is not only functional, but aberrant: the accumulation of junkyards at the edges of our cities, the flight of the rich to the suburbs, the rotting of great cities from the center, all attest to the fact that social mobility is not solely a beneficial phenomenon. The neo-nomadism of modern man is also without roots or focus. The lowered price of tolerance due to an excess of confrontations results in cynicism and in indifference.

Organized concentration? It too has its pathology. Our cities suffer simultaneously from bureaucratic over-organization and under-administration. Today's modern city is like an uncontrolled cancerous phenomenon; man finds his destiny there to be at the same time cumbersome and dispersed; in the place of generalized constraint, of the surplus-repression described by Herbert Marcuse, it is also the place of fragmentation of the personality.

The image of human energy? We have described it as an image of our own energy, but this energy, insofar as it is dominated by technology, risks losing itself in an empty futurism, in a useless Prometheanism, through loss of memory. All technological themes are futuristic, without tradition; technological progress cumulates by destroying its past. It is true that the "old cities" are also cities of art, sometimes veritable museums. The city is thus an "exchange agent" in another sense than previously mentioned: it exchanges tradition for projection of the future. But, insofar as the element which dominates the construction of the city is technological, the city also risks being the place where man perceives the absence of all collective and personal projects, the meshing of means in the absence of ends, and the loss of meaning.

We must bear in mind the city's ambiguity and ambivalence as we continue to reflect on that therapeutic action for which the cultural and intellectual societies (and, with these and among them, the ecclesiastical communities) are responsible.

THE RELATION BETWEEN SECULARIZATION
AND URBANIZATION

Let us recall some of the fundamental notions of secularization. We mean by secularization an institutional phenomenon: the emancipation of most human activities from the influence of ecclesiastical institutions. In this first sense, secularization is synonymous with laicization: the community no longer coincides with the parish, political authority dissociates itself from religious authority. This transfer of power from the churchman to the civil servant and politician has been marked by a series of crises in which communities, hospitals, and schools have been successively affected.

Urbanization and Secularization

In a second sense secularization is characterized by the erasing of the distinction between the spheres of the sacred and the profane. This distinction, applying to time (religious and non-religious holidays), space (holy places and public buildings), social roles (the priest and the layman), the world-view (the heavens and the earth), the emotions (piety and justice) has tended to disappear for modern man. Its disappearance characterizes modernity as such. To this loss of distinction is connected the dissolution of peculiarly religious traditions, which today have become merely cultural provincialisms resistant to the universal industrial society.

Behind these two preceding phenomena may be discerned a fundamental factor of an anthropological nature: the elevation of man to the position of autonomous subject of his history. This phenomenon has often been described as the coming to maturity of the adult. Ultimately it can be described as the elevation of a religious man, in the sense intended by Bonhoeffer in predicting the coming of a religionless time, a time in which man has no religion whatsoever.[2]

If such is the macroscopic description of secularization, how is it connected with the city-phenomenon? One could call it the effect as easily as the cause. The city accelerates secularization even though the latter is the cultural condition of its possibility. Thus man in the anonymous community, as we found in our first point, is certainly a secularized man; for him external relations prevail over internal ones. Mobility accelerates secularization by breaching the enclosure of traditional societies and condemning men to a thorough assimilation with one another. Organization is equally a secularization factor in that it requires social roles to be presented as essentially lay roles. As they become less and less "orders" with a traditional and sacral foundation, i.e., institutions with mystical origins in the depth of the past, they become more and more functional relations, non-traditional, claiming no origin and no ultimate meaning. They are directed toward the future more than they are rooted in the past; they make no claim to give an ultimate meaning to life; they are disjoint and not encompassing. All these points have been underlined by Harvey Cox. Thus the profane, radically secularized nature of the city's image is self-evident; the city is truly the world which the gods have fled and where man is delivered unto himself, to the responsibility of total expediency.

TOWARD A THEOLOGY OF CULTURE

It would be idle to try to articulate directly, on the basis of this description, an ecclesiological reflection that raises the question of what the task of the church can possibly be in the age of secularization and urbanization. *It is today necessary to juxtapose a theology of culture between sociology and ecclesiology.* One must indeed say that everything—or nearly everything—remains to be done in this interval. This is why Harvey Cox's work *The Secular City* represents a pioneering work in spite of its improvised character.

Harvey Cox initially poses the excellent question of whether Christian preaching, in order to accept the fundamental themes of secularization, must root these concerns in the very basis of this preaching, that is in the Old Testament and the New Testament. This is surely the *preliminary question*; in this sequence of investigation the theology of culture re-captures the hermeneutic debate, for the manner of *reading* Scripture is played off against the manner of *reading* contemporary culture. If it is true that the hermeneutic problem is determined by the cultural distance which separates our times from those where "these things have been said," there is still a relation between realizing the original preaching in to-day's world and discerning biblical sources of the secularization process. This is why everything is in play at the same time, in a complete reciprocity of biblical understanding and the understanding of our time.

Such is the foundational structure on which can subsequently be built a theology of development, a theology of responsible society, i.e., a theology of revolution (but our present discussion is less directly concerned with this aspect).

Harvey Cox finds three leitmotifs, which can produce what I myself call a receptive framework for a theology of the secular city: *disenchantment of nature, desacralization of politics, deconsecration of values.*

Disenchantment of nature: the Old Testament in particular should reveal this deep-seated intent to demythologize nature and consequently to offer nature to man's initiative and responsibility. The struggle against the Baals, gods of nature and lords of the earth; the proclaiming of a God who has no image, in particular none in the stars or in the forces of nature; the proclaiming of a God who has only a name but no cosmic base; the preaching of a God who inaugurates and accompanies a history more than he consecrates nature; all these themes correspond to an anthropology in which man, the giver of names, is called upon to dominate nature. Consequently what Max Weber calls the "disenchantment of nature" marks not only the dissolution of religion in contemporary culture but also the flowering of an originally biblical theme.

Desacralization of politics: the Exodus can actually be understood as a break with the sacral politics of the Pharaohs. The history of Israel is not noted for kings enthroned and consecrated but for prophets, scribes and Pharisees. In spite of efforts to give themselves a political structure comparable to that of their powerful neighbors, Israel never succeeded in constituting "divine" politics. Thus it achieved its true destiny which had been prefigured in the act of rupture of the Exodus: the New Testament gives a first fulfillment to this non-divine politics by linking the Passion of Christ to the Roman trial at law, that is, to the culpability of politics. The State-made-divine belonged henceforth to the grandeurs and dominions which had been vanquished on the cross.

Deconsecration of values: the struggle against idols, which culminates in the Second Isaiah,[3] has numerous ethical implications. Remember how the Second Isaiah belittles idols: you take a log, you cut

186

it in two; with half you warm yourself, with the other you make a god. Nietzsche would not reject this interpretation of the birth of value: man preserves and expands his will, and projects his values to heaven as ideal, all with the same wood. We are thus sent back to the historical invention of values; the Gospel gives only one absolute, love, but gives neither taboo nor interdiction. This situation forces us to accept our responsibility for the interhuman and profane constitution of an ethic.

Such is the foundational structure of a theology of culture. On this base can be *erected two stages*: *first a theology of social change, and then a theology of responsible control.*

The theology of social change lets us respond to the first two points of our description: the expansion of the sphere of relations and the acceleration of mobility. If the previous analysis of the fundamental intentions of the Bible is accurate, it is possible both to accommodate positively the phenomenon of secularization and to recognize the worth for us in what at first glance leaves us shaken and disturbed: the breaking of traditions, the availability for new contracts, the opening toward the future, the acceptance of the other. Two points especially deserve consideration for they constitute the critical node in our acceptance of "modernity": the reign of anonymity and that of the neo-nomadism, previously mentioned, both of which seem self-preserving and self-aggrandizing.

The mobility to which we seem condemned should not surprise us; were not the Jewish people nomadic before they established themselves in a land and,

above all, in holy places, in a temple? The despatializa-
tion of God brought about by the theology of "name,"
did not find its fulfillment in the Hebraic culture;
could it be that only in our culture all the implications
of this "non-place" nature of God became meaningful?
Did not Jesus himself have the misfits, the impious,
the "reprobates" for his real audience? Is not the
famous declaration of Paul that "there is neither
Jew nor Greek, there is neither bond nor free, there
is neither male nor female; for ye are all one in
Christ Jesus"[4] now being exemplified by the inces-
sant assimilation of the great cities? And does not
itinerancy, which is so closely bound up with a
theology of hope, demonstrate the priority of the
category of the future over that of the present and
the past in spite of the inertia of the establishment?
During the time of feudal civilization, of the small
town, Christianity had been respatialized; the theme
of itinerancy had been applied to the trip to a heavenly
kingdom, in order to justify establishment here
below. No theology of social change is possible unless
we return to the radical theme that we are itinerants
through and through; Christian preaching has always
said it, but Christendom had always located this
mobility "elsewhere." We have made foreigners
into aliens; we have made for ourselves an existence
which is culturally and spiritually sedentary. This
is why our eschatology has remained mythological
through and through: we have not been capable of
incorporating a profane interpretation of it into our
vision of the future.

The theme of anonymity adds more difficulties.
It strikes directly at the classical theologies, and,

perhaps even more strongly, at Protestant ones as
well. Although the Catholics attached their theology
to ontologies and finally to cosmologies (we recall
the "proofs of the existence" of God drawn from
the movement), Protestant theology is bound up with
the personalist theme of the "I-thou" relation. From
Luther to Bultmann, this relation has resisted demyth-
ologization; Bultmann in particular holds that the "I-
thou" relation is analogous at base and is not at all
mythological. Today we may wonder at what point
this relation ceases to be solely a member of the
class of God-man relations; not all is personalized
in the being-man. As Meister Eckhart and a number
of mystical thinkers said, not all is personalized
in the being-God either. It cannot be doubted that,
man being what he is, there is something human which
cannot be appropriated to a personal subject. Language
is the most striking example of this; the institution
in all its forms is another. Now human relations,
especially as experienced in the city, demonstrate
that the problem of the *socius* does not reduce to
the problem of the neighbor; otherwise, the rich,
full notion of the neighbor would encompass and
assimilate both the relation to the *socius*, which
is superlatively anonymous, and the relation of friendship and love, which is superlatively personal.
The good Samaritan of the parable did not enter into
an "I-thou" relationship at all: he treated the man
he met, if I may say so, functionally: he dressed
his wounds, led him to lodging, paid the bill; no one
ever tells us that he made a friend of him. One
might even wonder, with Harvey Cox, if it is not the
"pre-urban ethos," the mentality of the village and

189

small town, which has made us exaggerate the "I-thou" relation as the sum of all possible relations among men and between God and man. The new distribution of human relations between the private and the public which we are witnessing today leads us to reconsider the collusion between personalist theology and the ethic of the village and small town. I am not saying that this theology should entirely disappear; I even think the opposite. I only say that it should be thought through again, and I agree quite heartily that the pathology of the city (to which Harvey Cox has perhaps not paid sufficient attention) warns us against a wholly naïve enthusiasm concerning our modernity. There is a theological "everybody-on-the-bandwagon-ism" which is worth no more than its twin enemy "assimilationism." To rethink a situation is not necessarily to "throw out the baby with the bathwater." But if we knew better how to conceive the relationships between the personal and the anonymous, between the existential and the institutional in the very constitution of man, we would be even more critical with respect to the naïve analogies which theology uses. After all, when Paul said: there is neither Jew nor Greek, there is neither slave nor free, there is neither male nor female, he was designating non-personalized roles on which level alone a work of institutional reconciliation is possible. The being-man, the becoming-man, is also involved in thoroughly undermining the interrelations of social "roles"; a certain theology of individual conversion has hidden from us the scope both of this undermining and of those new beginnings, the labor pains of which are being felt by all humanity.

The second stage of this theology of culture will be constituted by a *theology of organization*. I would personally tend to give it as important a place as the theology of social change. Harvey Cox has particularly developed the latter, beginning with his reflections on anonymity and mobility, under the designation of a theology of the future and of hope. No doubt a European, whether Western or Eastern, would be more sensitive to this task which counterbalances the previous one. For the pathology of nomadism, of rootlessness and loss of memory (which I personally stress much more strongly than Harvey Cox) also finds its therapy in responsibility at the level of organization. In this respect, our most urgent task is to cure ourselves of all recrimination against organization as such; we are on a "reactionary" decline, socially, politically, and theologically, such that we dream, if not of forest man, at least of village man, the man of shop and farm. All the lamentations over the separation of work and family, the distantiation of roles and the fragmentation of the personality, bear witness to the fact that we are still prisoners of this "Protestant ethic" which Max Weber has shown to be tied (reciprocally) to capitalism. Protestantism, freeing itself with respect to the Middle Ages, soon bogged down in a theology of small-town burghers; it sanctified the figure of the business entrepreneur, competitor in a competitive market, at the same time that it sanctified labor as a personal vocation and thrift as asceticism. Thus the American Puritan has become the Protestant, as the corporation had been the Catholic. These two images are today in ruins; there is no longer time to try to preserve the personal garden of our soul against public existence. Our purpose in being social-Christians is to understand that a theology centered around the other, around the unknown neighbor, must take over the problems of organization and recapture the humanity of man at the very level of the organizations. That dream of the great nineteenth-century socialist utopians, the reconciliation of man and the product of his labor at the level of the immediate relation between the individual and his work is no longer even in question; it is rather in terms of democratic control or popular control of enterprise, of decision centers, of the state, of the international community, that a theology of responsible control must function. Thus we will actually be contemporaneous with the second or third industrial revolution in which we are taking part: that in which the business entrepreneur is subordinated to the organization man, and then that in which the owner of the means of production is subordinated to the technocrat who, by virtue of his technical competence, is today in a position to maneuver the owners themselves. This world is the one which must be "humanized," and not a world already dead. But we must admit that everything is yet to be done. Industrial democracy exists nowhere in the world. Democratic control of production, information and distribution is in effect nowhere in the world. The main theological theme would be this: liberty is not confined to that state where an individual "works out alone his own salvation," but also is to be sought where, by means of responsible control directed toward the common good, he feels himself "at home" in the community of men. As this point connects up with reflections developed elsewhere concerning the prospective and the perspective, I will content myself with referring the reader to this study.[5]

FROM THEOLOGY OF CULTURE TO ECCLESIOLOGY

Only when we have passed through theology of culture can we turn to the occupation of *ecclesiology*. But even within the very bounds of this ecclesiology, we must put aside discussions concerning the parish and other ecclesiastical organizations into which we tend to rush headlong. Before reflecting on the organization of and the organizations within the church, we must reflect on its *function*. This reflection connects up quite directly with the preceding one concerning the tasks of a theology of culture. Here ecclesiology is narrowly subordinated to the three themes which we just developed. This subordination is justified: the church is not primarily an institution but God's people; such a people is defined by its task of liberation and not by the structures which it assumes. These latter must be exactly proportional to its task.

Taking as his leitmotif that the church is "God's avant-garde," Harvey Cox organizes around the three ministries, i.e., the three services, its present task: to announce, to reconcile, and to make hope manifest in the community. Taking the three corresponding Greek words—*kerygma* or proclamation, *diakonia* or healing by reconciliation, *koinonia* or eschatological communion—he speaks of the triple function, kerygmatic, diakonic, and communal, of the church. I find no difficulty in adopting this analytic framework.

193

The church announces: this means first of all that it teaches us to recognize the time in which we live, to recognize its dangers and its tasks, its opportunities and its obstacles. This is what is essential for us in Jesus' preaching against the authorities. We announce that, in Christ, God has defeated the authorities. That means two things: first, that nothing is inevitable. In the face of resignation by all those who believe themselves delivered over to blind mechanisms, we must "defatalize" changes now in progress and show people that calculation and forethought create choices and responsibilities (which I have shown in my reflection on the prospective). But we must also affirm that meaning can always be found in the face of the contemporary threat of the absurd. Let us thus recapture in our own way the images of the Exodus and of Easter. Let us repeat after St. Paul, "Where sin abounds, grace superabounds."[6] We must witness to an economy of overabundance, that of sense over nonsense. It is the function of the church to discern this surplus of sense over nonsense, in the very face of the processes of decay, of cancerization in the modern city. Thus let us always return to man the responsibility for what appears to result from external forces, from non-human powers. Such is the crux of what could be called the preaching to *the world*, of which the preaching addressed to the faithful must remain a mere preliminary stage.

The therapeutic task can be understood from what has been said before concerning the pathology of the city. If it is true that one of the fundamental ministries of Christ was to exorcise demons (which ministry

Christ never distinguished from the fight against
legalistic constraints in his debate with the scribes),
the modern way of reviving the ministry of exorcism
is to apply the vigilance of the church to the neo-
formations, to the phenomena of canceration and in
general to the pathological products which stem from
the modern world. The ministry of the church is
here essentially a ministry of communication, applied
to the cleavages, to all the various kinds of divisions
found in the modern city, to the tendencies toward
fragmentation and dissociation of the personality
itself. Here is the true diakonia. It consists not in
supplementing society where it is deficient, although
certainly it must spend a great deal of time on
hospitals, caring for the sick and the poor which
society ignores or abandons. It is not restricted
to compensation; it applies to the centers of decision, to the major functioning points of the city, where
the processes of integration and disintegration intersect. It is here that a theology of itinerancy and
responsible control are to be applied. How can the
church be God's vanguard if the Christian individual
remains in the rear guard of historical development,
if all his compassion and all his deepest feelings
are turned toward the lost paradise and not toward
the kingdom to come? Once again the necessity of
joining a theology of responsible control to that of
itinerancy and hope cannot be overemphasized.

*The third function, appropriately the communica-
tive one,* cannot be isolated from the two preceding
ones. The church cannot manifest hope, cannot show
itself as God's vanguard if it is reduced to a middle-
class club concerned with the maintenance of homoge-

neity among its members. It must be emphasized
that there is no church in a community in which no
reconciliation is in progress. Once more, the words
of Paul,—there is neither Jew nor Greek, there is
neither bond nor free, there is neither male nor
female—do not constitute merely one secondary case
in point, among others, of unity in Christ; they designate the very center of anthropology and ecclesiology,
the place of their origin. "Man" is not a "such" plus
a "such," but rather "the humanity of man"; and the
humanity of man is being realized so long as the
Jew, the Greek, and the Barbarian are involved in
a process of reconciliation; hence the advent of
man. At the same time, by the very operation of the
gesture of reconciliation, a community is possible.
By this act the church rejects the model of the village
parish or the residential parish of the pre-industrial
age. Today we need ecclesiastical forms which take
into account the non-residential aspects of human
relation, of social intercourse. Above all we need
ecclesiastical forms which allow us to exercise the
ministry of reconciliation while at the same time
we announce the existence of meaning across the
fissures of the metropolis.

However, let us not draw from these reflections
the premature conclusion that the time of the residential parish is over. The new motivations which
appear relate to old ones; in particular, the response
to nomadism and anonymity gives concrete communities based on neighborhood proximity a second
chance. But it would be an error to believe that the
communal function of the church exhausts itself in
perpetuating—or even rejuvenating—this form of

congregation. I think it likely that the best chance for the traditional parish is in being one ecclesiastical modality among others. The non-parish will save the parish. We shall have to learn to see the face of the church wherever the ministries of announcement, of diakonia, and of concrete community confront the city as a whole, such as the modern world has made it; that is, the secular city.

NOTES

1. This study is inspired by Harvey Cox's *The Secular City* and refers freely to that work.

2. Dietrich Bonhoeffer, *Letters and Papers from Prison*, ed. Eberhard Bethge (New York: The Macmillan Co., 1967). *Ed.*

3. Also known as Deutero-Isaiah, the pseudonymous author of chapters 40-55 (and perhaps also 55-66) of the Biblical Book of Isaiah; distinguished from Proto-Isaiah, or simply Isaiah, the presumed historical Isaiah who wrote chapters 1-39. The reference here is to Isaiah 44:9-20. *Ed.*

4. Galatians 3:28. *Ed.*

5. "Prospective et Planification." Dialog with Piette Massé, *Cahier de Villemétrie*, no. 44.

6. Romans 5:20. *Ed.*

PART III

POLITICS AND THE STATE

10

ADVENTURES OF THE STATE
AND THE TASK OF CHRISTIANS

THE DOUBLE BIBLICAL "READING" OF THE STATE

IT IS OF DECISIVE IMPORTANCE FOR A CHRISTIAN IN-
terpretation of the State that the writers of the New
Testament have bequeathed us not one but two read-
ings of political reality: one, that of St. Paul, which
offers a difficult justification, the other that of St. John,
which offers an obstinate mistrust. For one, the State
has the face of the magistrate; for the other, it is the
face of the beast.

Thus it is first of all necessary to outline these
two faces and preserve them both as two contemporary
possibilities in each State which confronts us.

St. Paul, addressing himself to the Christians of
the empire's capital—who were little inclined to
acknowledge a meaning in a pagan power, foreign to
the Good News, and moreover involved in the process

Translated by Michael Gordy

which had resulted in the violent death of the Master
—invites his correspondents to obey not out of fear,
but by reason of conscience: the State which carries
the sword, which punishes, is "instituted" by God
and for the "good" of the citizens. And yet that
State occupies a very odd and precarious position
in the economy of salvation: the apostle has just
celebrated the grandeur of love—love which creates
reciprocal bonds ("love each other reciprocally
with a tender and fraternal affection")—love which
forgives and which renders *good for evil*. Now,
the magistrate does not do that: between him and the
citizens, the relation is not reciprocal; he does not
forgive; he renders evil for evil.

His title is not one of love, but of justice; nor is the
"good" that he serves the "salvation" of mankind,
but the maintenance of "institutions." Through him,
one might say, a violent pedagogy, a coercive education
of men as members of the historical communities that
the State organizes and directs, is carried out.

St. Paul does not say (and perhaps does not know)
how that *penal* pedagogy is connected to the charity
of Christ: he knows only that the established order
(*taxis* in Greek) realizes an intention of God concerning the history of men.

And at the same time that he attests to that divine
meaning in the institution of the State, St. Paul re-
serves the possibility of an inverse reading, for the
State, at the same time that it is an "institution," is
also a "power." In line with the more or less mythical conceptions of the epoch, St. Paul imagines a
more or less personalized demon standing behind
each political grandeur. Now, these powers have
already been conquered on the Cross—at the same

time as Law, Sin, Death and other powers—but are *not yet* annihilated. This ambiguous status ("already" but "not yet") about which O. Cullman has written decisively, very well illuminates the theological meaning of the State: willed by God as an institution, halfway from condemnation and destruction as a power, on the whole insecure in the economy of salvation and (on reprieve) until the end of the world.

Thus it is not astonishing that in another historical context, where the evil of persecution wins out over the good of law and order, it is the face of the "beast" which serves as the symbol of evil power. Chapter 13 of Revelation describes a beast wounded, probably mortally, but whose wound is temporarily healed; the power of the beast is not so much that of an irresistible force as that of seduction: the beast works wonders and demands the adoration of men; it is by falsehood and illusion that he enslaves. (In Plato's obviously kindred description of the "tyrant," the latter reigns only through the "sophist" who first twists language and perverts belief.)

This double theological pattern is full of meaning for us: we henceforth know that it is not possible to adopt for ourselves either a religiously motivated anarchism under the pretext that the State does not confess Jesus Christ, or an apology for the State in the name of "Be obedient to the authorities." The State *is* this dual-natured reality, simultaneously instituted and fallen.

THE DOUBLE HISTORY OF POWER

It is thus with this *double* guide that one must orient himself politically. The modern State simultaneously progresses along the line of the "institution" (what St. Paul called *taxis*) and along the line of "power," of seduction and of threat.

On the one hand we can indeed say that there is progress of the State in history; it is even admirable that through so many tears and so much blood, the legal and cultural achievements of humanity have been able to be saved, reaffirmed, and carried farther, in brief that humanity continues beyond the fall of empires, like a single man who continuously learns and remembers. This perpetuation of humanity, fostered by the "institution," is a sort of historical verification of the rash affirmation of St. Paul that all authorities are instituted by God.

I will give four *signs* of this institutional growth of the State through history:

The State is a reality that tends to evolve from an autocratic to a constitutional stage. All States were, of course, born from the violence of land-grabbers, warriors, captors of dowries and inheritances, enslavers of the people, unjust conquerors; but we see *force* tending toward *form*, making itself durable while making itself legitimate, involving ever more groups and individuals in the exercise of power, organizing discussion, and submitting to the control of its subjects. Constitutionality is the legal expression of the movement by which the *will* of the State stabilizes itself in a *law* which defines power, distributes it, and limits it. Certainly States succumb to violence, through wars and dictatorships, but the legal experience lasts; another State elsewhere inherits and continues it. However slow and restrained it may be, the movement of de-Stalinization, the liberalization of Soviet power, does not escape the effects of this

204

tendentious law in which I, for my part, see one of the verifications of the position of St. Paul on the State.

A second sign of this institutional growth of the State is the rationalization of power through the instrumentality of the administration. One does not reflect enough on the importance of this fact, as characteristic of the modern State as is legality. A State worthy of the name must today be a power capable of organizing a body of functionaries who not only execute its decisions but who also elaborate on them without yet having the political responsibility for them. The existence of the public administration as a neutral political body has radically transformed the nature of politics; it is in it that a part of the function of the magistrate is realized, namely, the part of power that is politically irresponsible. This development of public administration (on which we judge in part the capacities of the young States recently born in Asia and Africa) is an extension of technical rationality, more precisely of the organization of labor in the industrial enterprise. Thus power, irrational in its demonic essence, is rationalized through legality, expressed in the constitution, and through technicality, expressed in the administration.

A third sign of institutional progress resides in the organization of public discussion in modern societies; as perverted and enslaved as it may be, public opinion is a new sort of reality which grew from a certain number of "political occupations" that Max Weber studied; militants and officers of parties and unions, journalists, specialists in opinion and in human relations, publicists, and editors of magazines are the administrators of a new reality, in its own way an institution: the organized form of public discussion. Perhaps the term "democracy" should be reserved as a designation of the degree of citizens' participation in power by means of organized discussion (rather than calling the *constitutional* stage which succeeds the autocratic stage "democracy").

Finally, *the appearance of large-scale planning* represents the recent form of the institution of the State. The rejection of chance in favor of foresight and long-term planning manifests in the social and economic sectors of the life of the community the same type of rationality as that which has long been triumphant in other sectors. When the State took for itself the monopoly of vengeance and constituted itself as the unique penal force of the community, it rationalized punishment; a table of penalties henceforth corresponds to a classification of infractions. In the same way the State has in its Civil Code defined the different "roles," their rights and their obligations—the role of father, husband, inheritor, buyer, contracting party, etc.; this codification rationalized and in that sense already planned social relations. The large-scale economic planning of the modern State is within the tradition of this double rationalization of the "penal" and the "civil" and is ascribable to the same institutional spirit.

I think it necessary to say all of that if one wants to give even the faintest shadow of meaning to what is happening before our eyes and to escape an irrationalism without limits, without bottom, and without criteria.

But at the same time as I say that, it is necessary to say one other thing, which shows the external ambiguity of political reality. All growth in the institution is also growth in power and in the threat of tyranny. The same phenomena that we have reviewed under the sign of rationality can also be reviewed under the sign of demonism.

Thus we have seen, simultaneously in Germany and in Russia, constitutions serve as an alibi for tyranny. The modern tyrant does not abolish the constitution, but instead finds there the surface forms and sometimes the legal means of his tyranny: the delegations of power, the plurality of offices, the special legislations, the special powers.

Central administration extended to all extremities of the social body does not prevent political power from being totally senseless, as one saw during the dictatorship of Stalin; on the contrary, it offers to the folly of the tyrant the technical means for an organized and lasting oppression.

The techniques of opinion, on the other hand, expose the public to ideologies that are both extreme in their themes and rational in their outlines. The parties become "machines" whose organizational complexities are matched only by the spirit of abstraction that infuses its slogans, its programs, and its propaganda.

Finally, the large-scale socialist plans give to the central power methods of pressure on the individual that no bourgeois State has succeeded in mustering; the monopoly of proprietorship of the means of production, the monopoly of employment, the monopoly of provisions, the monopoly of financial resources and therefore of the means of expression, of scientific research, of culture, of art, of thought—all these monopolies concentrated in the same hand make the modern State a considerable and fearsome power. It is quite useless to think that the government of persons is in the process of turning into the administration of things, because all advancement in the administration of things (and one supposes that planning is one such advancement) is also an improvement in the government of persons. The distribution of great financial resources through a plan (investments and consumption, well-being and culture, etc.) represents a series of global decisions which concern the life of individuals and the *meaning* of their life: a plan is an ethics in action and thereby a means of governing men.

All these threats are suggestive, as are also the resources of reason, of order and justice that the State develops in unfolding the history of power. *What makes the State a great enigma is that these two tendencies are simultaneous and together form the reality of power. The State is, among us, the unresolved contradiction of rationality and power.*

OUR DOUBLE POLITICAL DUTY

Is it necessary, before drawing the inferences for action from this double reading of political reality, to recall two essential rules?

First rule: it is *not legitimate* (nor even possible) to *deduce* a politics from a theology, for every political commitment is formed at the point of intersection of a religious or ethical *conviction* with *information* of an essentially profane character, with a situation which defines a limited field of possibilities and available means, and with a more or less hazardous choice. It is not possible to eliminate from political action the tensions which arise from the confrontation of these diverse factors. In particular, conviction, when not controlled by a reflection on the possible, would tend to require the impossible to exist by requiring perfection: for if I am not perfect in everything, I am perfect in nothing. On the other hand, the logic of means, not controlled by a meditation on ends, would easily lead to cynicism. Purism and cynicism are the two limits between which political action extends, navigating with its guilt calculated between the morality of all or nothing and the technique of the feasible.

Second rule: political commitment has meaning not for the church but for the believers; that appears clear in principle, but it is not yet clear in fact. Churches as such are cultural realities which count in the balance of power, and there is always more or less a politics of the church, unacknowledged, residual, shameful; that is why the secularity of the State is not yet established; we are witnesses to the agony of political and clerical Christianity, and this never-ending agony demoralizes believers and non-believers.

Thus it is under the hypothesis of the political responsibility of the individual Christian that it is now necessary to draw the conclusions of the preceding contradictory analysis.

If that analysis is true, it is necessary to say that we ought *simultaneously* to improve the political institution in the direction of greater *rationality* and to exercise vigilance against the *abuse of power* inherent in State power.

For what *institutional improvements* are we particularly responsible today?

We have first, it seems to me, to pursue *constitutional evolution in a reasonable way*, i.e., in a way which takes into account the appearance of new nations in the geographical area controlled by the French State. The most important problem in French politics is that of transforming the centralizing state, inherited from the monarchy and from the Jacobin Republic, into a *federal State capable of reassembling on an egalitarian basis the nations which have grown up within its frontiers*. Such an invention of new structures would be a true promotion of rationality, because it would consist of adapting the constitutional reality to the historical, cultural, human reality of the modern world. The choice is imperative; either we shall do it and new bonds will be formed with the peoples abroad, or else we shall not do it, and these people will shape their destiny outside of us, even against us.

We have next to *renew the life of the parties*. One cannot say that the experiment of multiple parties should be condemned and that their pluralism reflects only the division into classes; a political instrument is necessary in order to make citizens discuss in order to form and formulate opinions. The existence of a number of parties would still be necessary even in a society without classes, because it translates the fact that politics is not a science, but an opinion. There is only one science—and even that is not completely true—but there are various opinions on the questions which concern the orientation of general politics. Thus it is in the interest of democracy that the parties survive the threats of death generated by the weight of the bureaucracy, the sclerosis of the political machines, the unreality of ideologies unrelated to the true problems of the time, the absurd proliferation and the pretentious dogmatism of French parties. *Two* parties would probably suffice if they were able to integrate many of the contradictions resolved in the concrete formulas of government, and if they maintained internally a permanent and free discussion. This is the essential condition of the restoration of public opinion.

We have next to invent new ways of getting the citizens to participate in power, other than the system of elections and parliamentary representations. We have to study here Yugoslavian, Polish and other endeavors in order to create a new representation of groups of workers or consumers. If an economy of work is intended which makes work the dominant economic category, only a politics in which workers were represented as workers would make of that economy of work a civilization of workers. Perhaps this task of inventing new modes of popular representation is to be combined with the renovation of parties; it is not only a question of defending democracy, but of spreading it.

Finally, it is necessary, as is often said, with a different meaning, to *strengthen the authority of the State*. This is not the first task, if by strengthening the authority of the State one means increasing the indirect power of various pressure groups on a

211

weak State with an unchanged centralizing structure resting on artificial parties without substance or internal democracy. This is, nevertheless, what is currently called "strengthening the authority of the State." Now, if that formula has a meaning, it signifies that civil power has authority over military power, over the police, and over the administration, that the power of decision belongs to the executive and not to the technocrats, that the executive is accountable only to the representatives of the people and not to pressure groups, beet growers or oil magnates.

All this action is reasonable and supposes that the State can be reasonable, that it is reasonable in so far as it is the State, and that it can become more and more reasonable. But this reasonable task, directed towards the goal of a reasonable State, does not exclude, but rather includes, an ever prepared vigilance, directed against the simultaneously growing threat of an unreasonable and violent State.

That vigilance takes several forms:

It is, first of all, *a critical vigilance* on the level of thought. Political philosophy, from Plato and Aristotle up to Marx, has never ceased developing the theme of the perversions or alienations of the politician. Now, this vigilance flags as soon as one begins to believe that political evil comes from outside the political sphere, from the struggle of classes or of groups, and that it suffices to have a good economy in order to have good politics. Constant thought about the evils peculiar to the politician, about the passions of power, is the soul of all political vigilance directed against the "abuse of power."

But that vigilance must also take the form of a *summons* and an *awakening*. It is sometimes necessary *to appeal from the State to the values on which it is grounded*. Every State rests on an implicit or tacit consent, on a "pact" which ratifies common beliefs, common ends, and a common good. (It is the "good" which St. Paul was speaking about when he said that the magistrate exercises constraint "for your good.") The State can and must be *judged* with regard to the values which *justify* it. Nor are the citizens ever absolved by the State from the service of these ideals; they have the duty to condemn the actions—the exactions, one ought to say— that are incompatible with these ideals. Protests against torture derive from this source. Ultimately such protests open up the possibility of illegal acts bearing witness to the "good" which grounds the State itself; these acts, negative in appearance, are in reality very positive: they reaffirm the ethical foundation of the nation and the State.

Finally, vigilance must take a specifically *political* form and *must be connected to the institutional reform* of which we have spoken. We have, in effect, to strengthen the State and, at the same time, to *limit* its power: that is the most extreme practical consequence of our entire analysis. It means that in the period in which we must extend the role of the State in economic and social matters and to advance along the path of the *socialist State*, we must also continue the task of *liberal politics*, which has always consisted of two things: to divide power among powers, to control executive power by popular representation.

To divide power means in particular to insure the independence of the judge that the politician tends to enslave. It is there that Stalinism has failed, for the tyrant would not have been able to purge and liquidate his political enemies without the complicity and servility of the judicial power. But the division of power implies perhaps an invention of new powers that the liberal tradition has not known. I am thinking in particular of the necessity to guarantee and even to institute the independence of cultural power, which in fact covers a vast domain: from the university (which has not yet found its proper position between dependence upon the executive and an anarchic liberty of a competitive type) to the press (which currently can choose only between the support of the State and the support of the capitalists), passing through scientific research, publishing, and the fine arts. The socialist State more than any other requires such a separation of powers, precisely because of its concentration of economic power; more than any other State, it needs the independence of the judge and that of the university and the press. If citizens have access only to the sources of information that the State provides, socialist power will ineluctably turn to tyranny; and the same will happen if scientific investigation and literary and artistic creation are not free.

But one can divide power only if one *controls* the executive power. And here I want to stress the erroneous nature of the dream—derived from anarchism and integrated into communism—of the withering away of the State. Certainly the repressive military and police apparatus of the bourgeois State may

214

wither away, but not the State *qua* power of organization and decision, *qua* monopoly of unconditioned restraint. In any case the State must strengthen itself before eventually withering away, and the problem is to prevent it from enslaving men during this no doubt long period in which it will be growing yet stronger. Now, control of the State is control by the citizens, by the workers, by the base; it is the upwards movement of sovereignty from below, in opposition to the movement from above down of government. This movement from below upwards must be willed, prepared, defended, and extended against tendency of power to eliminate the forces from which it comes. That is the whole meaning of the liberal struggle.

I have said that there is no Christian politics, but rather a politics of the Christian as a citizen. In finishing it is necessary to say that there is *a style of the Christian in politics.*

This style consists in finding the legitimate place of politics in life: elevated but not supreme. It is in an elevated place, because politics is the first education of the human race in order and justice; but it is not in the supreme place, because this violent pedagogy educates man for outer liberty, but it does not save him, it does not radically liberate him from himself, it does not render him "happy" in the sense of the Beatitudes.

This style further consists in seriousness of commitment, without the fanatacism of a faith; for the Christian knows that he is responsible for an institution which is an intention of God with regard to the history of men, but he also knows that this institution

215

is prey to a vertigo of power, to a desire for divinization which adheres to its body and soul.

Finally, this style is characterized by a vigilance which excludes sterile criticism as much as millenarian utopianism.

A unique intention animates this style: to render the State possible, true to its own destiny, in that precarious interval between the passions of individuals and the preaching of reciprocal love which pardons and returns good for evil.

11

FROM MARXISM TO CONTEMPORARY COMMUNISM

To WHAT EXTENT IS CONTEMPORARY COMMUNISM, guided by the Party and bound to the political destiny of the Soviet Union, the sole and legitimate heir of Marx and, more precisely, of his written works? This question is preliminary to all discussions bearing either on Marxism or on orthodox communism.

I would like to show that between Marx and Stalin there has emerged a considerable gap, and that Marxism, from the one to the other, has progressively *closed itself up*: it is understood increasingly dogmatically and mechanistically, political Machiavellism has suffocated it as free thought, and its eschatology has been reduced to a technical aspiration. And yet Marxism is greater than its Stalinist projection.

Translated by Kirk Augustine

We shall attempt now to understand the movement by which Marxism has become increasingly crystallized.

THE AMPLITUDE OF MARXISM

It is to the philosophy of the young Marx that we must return: it constitutes in truth the *obscurity of Marxism*. Its own roots extend back into the theology of the young Hegel.

Indeed it was in the *Early Theological Writings*[1] that Hegel's theme of alienation, in the sense of the loss of human substance in something other than oneself, was taken up. The Jew was initially for the young Hegel the model of that consciousness which voids itself by emptying into an alien Absolute. But Hegel attempted throughout his life to show the fecundity of this "unhappy consciousness," at least if it is gone beyond, surpassed, and integrated into the absolute knowledge in which consciousness and its Other are reconciled. Feuerbach took up the original theme once again and converted it into radical atheism: if man is annihilated in God, his task is to "recover in his heart that being that he had rejected"; if God appears when man is annihilated, then God must disappear in order that man may reappear.

It was in the extension of this atheism that that of Marx was constituted: Marx was an atheist and a humanist before being a communist. "The workers' religion is Godless because it seeks to restore the divinity of man" (letter to Hardman); it is the (positive) vision of man as the generator of his own history that orients the (negative) critique of aliena-

218

tion. It would be impossible to overestimate the importance of the texts in the *Economic and Philosophical Manuscripts*[2]: there we see the critique of religion, complete at its inception, searching for an economic foundation. It is the *production* of man by man which renders the idea of creation unacceptable; "Since, however, for socialist man, *the whole of what is called world history* is nothing but the creation of man by human labor, and the emergence of nature for man, he, therefore, has the evident and irrefutable proof of his *self-creation*, of his own *origins*."[3] The recovery by man of his own loss makes the existence of God superfluous.

But this text already introduces the specifically Marxian factor: the interpretation of man as a *laborer* and, as such, as the producer of his own existence. It is here that alienation according to Hegel and Feuerbach begins to be put into its economic and social context.

One can thus already at this stage speak of a materialism; Marxist materialism antedates the theory of class struggle. It signifies that alienation derives from the material life of man and proceeds to his spiritual life. But this materialism appears when the relation of the spiritual life to the material life is conceived most fully as a "reflection." The *German Ideology*[4] provides here decisive evidence. It is the most materialistic text of Marx: "Ideas emerge continually from the life process;"[5] the nature of men must be found "not as they conceive themselves, but as they are, that is to say, acting, producing."[6] Ultimately one must say that "there is no history of politics, of law, of science, of art, of religion"[7]; " . . . such is the true materialism of real society."[8]

It is this materialism that seeks to make itself scientific through a history of *money*; in the texts prior to the *Manifesto* money is already the instrument of the material alienation of man: to understand its mechanism is already to de-alienate oneself. Thus a new critique is born, no longer a critique of consciousness by consciousness, but a *real* critique of *real* conditions. The most extreme point of this critique is the last of the *Theses on Feuerbach*: "Philosophers have merely *interpreted* the world in different ways; the point, however, is to *change* it."[9]

The *Economic and Philosophical Manuscripts* summarize the situation well by calling for "the positive suppression of all alienation, and the return of man from religion, the family, the State, etc., to his *human*, i.e., social, life."[10] The text adds " . . . religious alienation as such occurs only in the sphere of *consciousness*, in the inner life of man, but economic alienation is that of *real life*, and its suppression, therefore, affects both aspects."[11]

Why speak of a Marxist obscurity with regard to these texts? Because this materialism is capable of several meanings. This materialism is not a materialism of the *thing*, but a materialism of *man*: it would be better to call it a realism. That man is a "producer" emphasizes that he is not nature or animality; moreover he does not "produce" only to live, but to humanize himself and to humanize nature. Nature itself appears as the "inorganic body of man."[12] Labor thus becomes a more-than-economic category; through it man expresses himself, enlarges himself, creates. We could say that Marx was pursuing, through work, the dream of innocence: the reconciliation of man with things and with others, and reintegration with himself.

That is why man's alienation is itself always more than economic: it is the over-all dehumanization of man. What the product of labor is, the laborer is not.[13] Before understanding the mechanism of surplus value, Marx knew what it meant for man to produce himself as a commodity. Alienation is disgraceful precisely because labor is for man the sole means of augmenting the value of natural products, his creative property, the sole and unchangeable measure of all things.[14] It is impossible to see how such a description could be possible without indignation, and thus without a specifically ethical moment of evaluation: "The *devaluation* of the human world increases in direct relation with the *increase in value* of the world of things."[15]

But if Marxism was, at its origin, more than economic, what then was it? Was it philosophy? Sociology? It seems to me that Marxism created a mode of thought that is to scientific economics what phenomenology is to psychology. There is perhaps no *mechanism* of which Marx was really the inventor. In the words of Bigo, "Marxism is not an explanation of mechanism, but an explanation of existence." Its science "does not aim at developing empirical laws or at finding better arrangements. It takes capital and value as existing situations of men and it sets itself the goal of showing their deep-seated opposition. Marxist science—lengthy developments will be necessary to render the initially misleading idea acceptable—is in reality a philosophy of man, a meta-physics of the subject, more precisely a meta-economics of capital and of value."[16]

It is because it is a question of a meta-economics that the Hegelian law of contradiction and reconciliation is salvageable in a dialectic of real men. The movement of humanity appears now as the passage from undifferentiated unity (primitive communism) to the class economy that is the antithesis of the preceding thesis; the synthesis is then a return to the thesis, but through "negation": from the class economy one retains the technology and suppresses the exploitation. Such a general view eludes all empirical verification. It is rather a question of clarifying through the *totality* of history each of its moments; the comprehension of this totality involves a sociological forecast, a judgment of economic and ethical values, and a maxim for action.

At the same time the exploitation of man by man which inaugurates the "negative" is neither a *moral evil* nor an *external fate*. It is not a dialectic external to man, a mechanistic determinism, but rather a movement of man: " . . . all the so-called history of the world is nothing but the production of man through human labor." Moreover, the division of labor necessarily produces the division into classes without there being any discernible guilt on the part of anyone: exploitation and alienation can't be analyzed into individual violences, into theft, into trickery, or into fraud. Everything happens as if humanity taken as a whole had preferred progress through suffering to happiness in stagnation.

This is why Marx cannot be considered a moralist, in spite of the role of indignation in the comprehension of economic evil and of his declarations in favor of the workingman. For the denunciations were not made at the level of men's intentions, but at the level of the production relations in which men are involved. This is the place to recall that the hero of Marx's works is not the capitalist, nor even the proletarian, but rather capital as the alienated part of man become a situation and a thing. Thus the comprehension of this situation, by Marx himself, for example, or by any man who discovers his alienation, is not a moral liberation, valuable for its purity, but a moment of the process by which history as a whole passes from alienation to freedom. The psychological and moral "conscience" is not the initiator of alienation, nor has it the responsibility for de-alienation: the "ethical" act which Marx's work constitutes takes its place in the field of forces that it describes. Such is the *dialectic*: human and yet not moral; governed by things, but by things that are a forgotten, abolished, alienated part of man.

As is evident, all this is very ambiguous and can develop into either a very complex humanism or a very crude materialism of a mechanistic and deterministic type.

THE PETRIFICATION OF MARXISM

The process of narrowing or crystallization to which we initially alluded has a three-fold origin: in Marx himself, in Lenin, and in the practice of the monopolistic Bolshevik party.

Marx is himself responsible for the lapsing of his materialism into crude, mechanistic, and thingish materialism. The anti-Hegelian polemic made him hold that his system was the inverse of German idealism: that would be the dialectic returned to its feet. But this materialism of opposition tends inevitably towards the theory of consciousness as a reflection. There is no doubt that Marx provided all the necessary footholds for that theory of his own interpretation of non-economic alienations: ideology is the reflection of economic alienation.

And yet, as Lukács saw, there was in the theory of "false consciousness" a profound theory of masks, of illusions, and of irreality that was quite different from the vulgar idea of reflection—for a reflection (in the water, in a mirror) is still a thing. We should consider the striking texts on the State in *On The Jewish Question*: "In the State . . . man is the imaginary member of an imaginary sovereignty . . . [he is] infused with an unreal universality."[17] The illusory, the unreal, false consciousness—these are distinctly different from reflections!

It was, finally on the occasion of these analyses worthy of Plato's *Sophist*—the unreal reality of the false consciousness!—that Marx sank into the crudest materialism. It was the symmetry of idealism and materialism and the purely polemic definition of the latter that made Marxism swing from a humanist realism to a historical materialism.

Lenin is responsible for two things:

a) Through his theoretical work, with *Materialism and Empirio-criticism* at its center, he gave the theory of consciousness and of ideology its most reductionist sense. His struggle against neo-Kantianism, against Mach, against the theories of consciousness conceived as the center and origin of meanings, put him in a polemical situation comparable to that of Marx against Hegelian idealism. At the same time Marxists were stressing the scientistic pretensions of the theory of value in the face of opposition from bourgeois economists; Marxism claimed victory on empirical grounds as a scientific theory of money, of crises, of the laws of the market. It willingly placed itself on the terrain of the scientistic positivism of the late nineteenth century. Now it is doubtful that Marxism is on its true terrain there, for its theory of value is a consequence of its theory of alienation and describes the alienated world. Materialism itself is a description of the loss of man in things; it isn't a scientific law, but the truth of a world without truth. All this implicit content of original Marxism is lost in the attempt to set it up as an objective science.

b) But it is perhaps the theory of the proletarian State and its neo-Machiavellism that bears the greatest responsbility in the petrification of Marxism. *State and Revolution* is in this regard a fundamental link in the history of dogmatic

Marxism. The State appears there, in opposition to the social contract theory, not as the organ of the general will, but as an instrument for the domination and oppression of one class by another. This exercise in lucidity, exposing the irreality of the State as law and its violence as power, becomes an apology for proletarian violence: since the State is fundamentally repressive and punitive, it is such a State that the proletarian revolution will wield against the enemies of the people. "The state, i.e., the proletariat organized as the ruling class,"[18] remains evil until it perishes.

> . . . at best [the state] is an evil inherited by the proletariat after its victorious struggle for class supremacy, whose worst sides the victorious proletariat will have to lop off as speedily as possible, just as the Commune had to, until a generation reared in new, free social conditions is able to discard the entire lumber of the state.[19]

We may wonder if this trafficking with violence has not reconstituted Marxism as a "false consciousness," as an "ideology." Again, with the *raison d'état*, there is the cunning of reason; again there is the secret, the lie, the cleverness, and the *non-transparence of action*, once the action is placed in the shadowy strategy of the proletarian State. More and more the entire domain of truth is congealed; the party *says* the truth on art, on science, on public and private morality.

The political philosophy of Marxism leads us to consider the last factor in Marxism's petrification: the practice of the monopolistic party. The idea that there exists a group of men who hold a monopoly on the interpretation of history in its entirety, the idea that this group of men constitutes the sole perspective on the totality—such ideas are the source of all the dogmatism that has congealed Marxism. This dogmatism of truth, itself linked to the political philosophy of Marxism-Leninism, boomerangs back to alter all the Marxist theses. Everything that had remained ambiguous in Marxism is decreed in an orthodox tone; the most dogmatic—the most "materialistic" and the least "dialectical"—regularly win out over the more complex, the more open. It is the end of the Marxist obscurity.

Does open Marxism still exist somewhere? Do its adherents—cut off from the party apparatus and from real power, separated from action and relegated to a bookish doctrine—have a future? It is a question of knowing what the audience is today for non-Stalinist, non-dogmatic Marxists who are not enmeshed in the party orthodoxy. Only the history of the coming decades will show if open Marxism can yet renew from the inside scholastic Marxism.

Christians should at least know that original Marxism is not less irreligious than contemporary communism. It is not less atheistic because it is more "humanistic" and less "materialistic." To the contrary, its radical humanism is perhaps closer to the origin from which atheism sprang: the conviction that man is the producer of his own existence.

NOTES

1. G. W. F. Hegel, *Early Theological Writings*. trans. T. M. Knox (Chicago: University of Chicago Press, 1948).

2. Karl Marx, *Early Writings*. trans. T. B. Bottomore (New York: McGraw Hill, 1963).

3. *Ibid.*, p. 166.

4. Karl Marx, *The German Ideology* (Moscow: Progress Publishers, 1964). [All references are to Vol. 1, pp. 23-510. *Eds.*]

5. *Ibid.*

6. *Ibid.*

7. *Ibid.*

8. *Ibid.*

9. Karl Marx and Friedrich Engels, *Selected Works in One Volume* (New York: International Publishers, 1970), p. 30.

10. Karl Marx, *Early Writings*, p. 156.

11. *Ibid.*

12. *Ibid.*, p. 127.

13. *Ibid.*, pp. 122-23.

14. *Ibid.*, p. 123.

15. *Ibid.*, p. 121.

16. Pierre Bigo, *Marxisme et humanisme: Introduction à l'oeuvre economique de Karl Marx*, 3rd ed. (Paris: Presses Universitaires de France, 1961), p. 1.

17. Karl Marx, *Early Writings*, pp. 13-14.

18. Karl Marx, *The Communist Manifesto.* Cited in V. I. Lenin, *Collected Works* (Moscow: Progress Publishers, 1964), Vol. 25, p. 402.

19. Friedrich Engels, Preface to the third edition of *The Civil War in France.* Cited in V. I. Lenin, *Collected Works*, Vol. 25, p. 453.

12

Socialism Today

IT IS DIFFICULT TO SPEAK OF SOCIALISM TODAY BECAUSE it is at one and the same time both the master word for hundreds of millions of men and a formidable ambiguity in our economical and political language. Does one mean by "socialism" the program of Western socialist parties or the authoritarian phase of development in Eastern communism prior to the withering away of the state? Is it vague demands of leftists around the world, or is it India and Guinea? What is the difference between socialism and neo-capitalism? Is socialism the doctrine of the "Founding Fathers" or the actual experience developed in the field? How can we avoid throwing together a reformist practice and a revolutionary phraseology? One might even be tempted to forego use of the term "socialism," on the grounds that it is worn out, that it is a part of the leftist logomachy, or that only worn-out analyses are repeated in its name. But then we

Translated by Françoise Bien

run the risk of "throwing out the baby with the bath water," the seed of hope with the chaff of words. How can we retain the *aims* and renew the *analyses*? My task is to identify once again these permanent aims.

THE ECONOMIC LEVEL: PLANNING

To begin with I shall define a first, purely economic level of socialism. By socialism we shall understand the transition from a market economy to a planned economy that is responsive to human needs and that is characterized by a transfer of the ownership of the means of production to collective or public entities.

This definition has three elements; it is their combination which allows for a discussion of socialism.

By "market economy" we mean an economy in which production and consumption are regulated by profits and *monied* needs. In a planned economy, on the contrary, economic decisions do not depend in the last resort on the possession of wealth; they are instead made by organizations representing the common interest whose fundamental purpose is the maximum satisfaction of real needs in the order of urgency. Seen this way, socialism represents the conquest of the economy by rationality, by the same rationality that was previously at work in technology and in the sciences. In a planned economy, the economic reality is in a way "constructed" by foresight and decisions.

When can we speak of *socialist* planning? The question is not as simple as it might appear. The desire for rationality existed and still exists outside

socialism: postwar Keynesian interventionism did
not call the private ownership of the means of production into question, but advocated only a rational
management of State interventions (monetary policy
allowing expansion, prudent growth of public investments, redistribution of tax monies, etc.). Between
that kind of interventionism and true socialism there
is a whole range of controlled economies characterized by all sorts of efforts to correct the worst
effects of capitalism in the light of the analyses
of the national accounts. Among these efforts we
find all sorts of remedial interventions and functional and limited plans that respect the capitalist
system's structures and institutions. Some of these
relate only to certain categories of properties, others
to groups of activities. In this case planning deals
with the different economic balances possible in
view of .diverse political choices. Thus planning can
coincide with an economy which can yet on the whole
be called a market economy. In these systems that
are mixtures of controls and of spontaneous economic actions, fundamental needs are no longer
satisfied only in so far as they are monied: the
prime motive of social utility wins out over that of
profit. Profit can even undergo a partial socialization through a distribution of benefits, through
special tax rates, or finally through social programs.

These mixed economies are threatened by inco-
herence: two kinds of logic—the logic of collective
benefits and that of individual benefits—are fight-
ing for dominance. Public enterprises have a tendency
to imitate private enterprises and, like them, to
pursue private aims. Furthermore, if the State is

dominated by representatives of the non-nationalized section of the economy, rather than by the workers, it is the capitalistic mentality which will be expressed even in the public section of the economy. Finally, we fear that planning, when it is devoid of a social aim, is only a means for a purely cybernetic management of the economy, a pure technique of balance and of expansion, removed from any consideration for real men. This is why a second characteristic must be added to the simple definition by economic rationality.

The second characteristic is the reference of the economic plan to human need. With this, one is dealing with a change in structure and in mentality, and not only with a change of functions: an over-all strategic view of economic action replaces the perspective and the interests of small economic units, a clear vision of priorities and of large-scale decisions involving man dominates the whole economic project. Thus already at this point the humanistic aspect of socialism, which we will discuss later, has appeared. The macro-decisions involved in planning have necessarily an ethical character: whether it be a matter of giving preference to cultural goods over material goods, to consumption over investment, etc., such questions are essentially concerned with the destiny of man.

The third characteristic is the collective appropriation of the means of production. This was the principal concern of the "founding fathers" of socialism. Why this change? Why is it that the collective appropriation of the means of production, which once was an aim, is today reduced to a means? The founders of socialism started from a theory of alienation of which the central idea was the direct exploitation of labor by the owner of capital (the Marxist theory of surplus-value is the best example of this theory of alienation).

Thus property appeared as the immediate means of depriving the worker of the product of his labor. The appropriation of the means of production appeared then as an expropriation. "Property is theft," Proudhon said. Today we are less sensitive to the direct effects of the right of property and to the immediate consequences of the legal status of the ownership of the means of production. The emphasis is now placed on the impact of property on the power of decision. In this regard property appears doubly as an obstacle: it is first of all an obstacle to regulation in accordance with the general interest. The irrational intervention of profit and of monied needs prevents the achievement of sizeable and regular growth rates. In the light of this first difficulty, property is criticized with the purely technocratic argument that it is an irrational economic phenomenon. On the other hand, property is responsible for the warping of planning into a pure technique of equilibrium and expansion. This second argument seems more humanistic than the preceding one, for it holds that it is property that prevents us from realizing the properly socialistic motive of the maximum satisfaction of human needs. With both forms of the argument, however, property appears less as a direct instrument of exploitation than as an obstacle to the rationality of planning and to the domination of the technocratic motive by the human motive.

This is how socialism appears, then, in this initial view. It is the idea that an organism moved by the motive of social gain is more rational than one which is dominated by the competition of economic units, each of which is pursuing its own profit. Socialism appears thus as the system which best allows the application of rationality to the interests of the community taken as a whole.

THE POLITICAL AND SOCIAL LEVEL:
DEMOCRATIC MANAGEMENT

Socialism must also be considered from the point of view of management, that is to say, of the participation of the greatest number of individuals in economic decisions. At this level the question is one of the realization of democracy in the economy. The goal of socialism is the reintegration of man into the economic and social mechanisms. Indeed the will to satisfy human needs in the most rational way is not enough to define socialism; we know full well that the often vague aspiration toward a more just, egalitarian, and communal society is the real soul of socialism. But this second goal lags far behind the first one. Everywhere rationality is on the march, but nowhere is the participation of the greatest number in economic decisions making progress. This is where socialism remains entirely to be achieved. Yet from the beginning socialism has opposed the administration of things by a technical oligarchy *à la* Saint-Simon and has aimed at a democratic administration of things, carried out in the name of the masses and controlled by them. We are today much clearer in this respect, for we have before our eyes the various pathological expressions of planning, especially Stalinist planning. The question is now asked: is the Stalinist monstrosity a symptom or an accident? Is it due to planning as such or to the special Russian circumstances: the initial poverty of the country, the external dangers, the imperatives of a too rapid industrialization, the personality of the dictator himself, the lack of a democratic past? The question remains and is not removed by the remark that capitalist industrialization was itself also very costly. One must measure carefully the political and human risks and costs of socialist planning. One must also lose the illusion that Marx still cherished when he wrote *The Poverty of Philosophy* in answer to Proudhon's *The Philosophy of Poverty*: "The working class in the course of its development will substitute for the old civil society an association which will exclude classes and with it their antagonism; there will be no more political power as such since political power is precisely the official sum of antagonism in civil society." We know today that the administration of things does not supersede the government of men but on the contrary reinforces it; *things* are themselves the result of human labor directed at the satisfaction of human needs. This is why the administration of things returns the government to questions of work and of the needs of men. This is also why economic power is ineluctably a government of men: the management of the operations of production is a form of the power of man over man. At least in its first period, the administration of things reinforces the government of men.

It must be confessed that there are dangers inherent in a planned economy: power is concentrated in fewer hands than in a capitalistic economy slowed down by its contradictions; everything in it is co-ordinated at the top, where the ultimate decisions are made by a limited number of men who have an almost limitless power over the collectivized wealth. Furthermore the material means of expression are in the hands of the ruling group. This group can impose a rigid orientation on labor and on the professions and exert a sort of authoritarian centralization of all choices. In order to assure itself of a long-term efficacity, the ruling group has the economic means to remove from itself the pressure of public opinion and to mechanically redirect public opinion itself.

These dangers inherent in a planned economy pose acutely the problem of industrial democracy. I shall review a few of them. First of all it appears necessary that planning be total in extension, but partial in intensity and that the decentralized units be multiplied. We may probably say that only a planning that is total in extension can be minimally constraining, for only choices on the largest scale can bring forth a series of subordinate choices that are relatively autonomous within the framework of those larger choices. At present, however, this is more a problem than a program.

How can we avoid the creation of a new slavery through bureaucracy? How can we, on the one hand, assure the necessary stability and continuity of economic power and, on the other hand, assure the participation of the lower classes in decisions in ways other than through a fictitious and *a posteriori* control which, in the case of the People's Democracies, does nothing but ratify decisions which come from the top? It is imperative to create representative organs for the discussion of fundamental choices. Political parties such as we know them today seem ill-adapted to this function, as they either represent special interest groups or combine divergent interests which neutralize each other, as is the case in the large American parties. It will be necessary to take a look at what the Yugoslavian producers' councils represent.

On a lower level the problem of the administration of the companies by the workers themselves must be posed. If the councils of workers do not have the power to accept or refuse higher production quotas, if no margin of choice in the direction of the company is left to them, if they have no share in the control over the director's execution of policies, one cannot really speak of a socialist economy. Ultimately the goal of socialism is the right of each producer to decide how at all levels the surplus of his work will be distributed and used. Socialism is the end of the non-freedom which is represented by need and the conquest of the positive freedom that participation in decisions at all echelons constitutes.

At this second level one can say that socialism is the system in which workers are the dominant social category; it is the system in which a democracy of labor exists side-by-side with planning. And this second task must not be postponed in the name of the first, for the more powerful and extended that the means of action available for the government of men are, the more democratic the institutions and the customs should be. The major danger of a socialist economy is that its whole machinery may come under the control of a privileged and dominant minority. This peril can be eliminated only by a radical socialization of the means of government themselves, and this contrary to the existence of a single party and to any system in which the trade unions are reduced to the simple function of diffusing propaganda or to the role of the welfare office.

THE CULTURAL LEVEL: SOCIALIST HUMANISM

At the third level, socialism is a *culture*.

This third definition is implied by the two preceding ones: if socialism gives precedence to real needs over profit and also over a pure technique of equilibrium and expansion, and if socialism implies the participation of the greatest number in economic decisions, then a whole conception of man is already traced out in this dual demand. It is in the humanism of socialism that its most fundamental and most stable aim lies. But what is to be understood here by humanism? In my opinion three things are to be understood:

We find once again in the forefront the oldest theme of the founding fathers' socialism: the theme of the de-alienation of human work. In spite of its profession of materialism, Marxism appears in this regard as a fundamental humanism; it is Marxism which has exposed the mechanism through which man loses his humanity and himself becomes merchandise, in the image of the fetishes he has projected on his own existence, the fetish of merchandise and of money. Here the profound meaning of Marxism appears: its materialism is the truth of a man without truth. This truth is purely phenomenological, by which I mean that materialism is a precise description of alienated

man. In this regard the removal of the criticism of
propriety which we discussed in the first part has
changed nothing in this descriptive truth. Capitalism's
power of alienation lies in the fact that it has, after
having recognized the economic function of work,
sacrificed its fundamental human meaning by subordinating it to the law of profit, to the law of things,
to the power of money. This is why we have never
had done with that power of denunciation as well as
of description which emanates from Marx's imposing
work. I shall come back to this later on: it is the
lasting task of a Christian theology of work constantly
to reconsider the Marxist theses on alienation and
de-alienation and to integrate them into a larger
modern anthropology.

The second theme of this humanism is that of man's
control over economic phenomena. And indeed a de-
alienation that was not the work of man himself but
of a bureaucracy or of an economic apparatus foreign
to each of the workers would only shift the alienation
from the economic into the political. This is why de-
alienation must be extended by what we earlier called
the socialization of the means of government. The
human import of this theme is as great as that of
the preceding one, because it means that there is no
socialism without the triumph of human responsibility
over blind mechanism, including those of politics,
of administration and of bureaucracy. If alienation
means that man has become a stranger to himself,
there are many roads leading to this alienation, and
socialism is in danger of creating new ones, under
the pretext of putting an end to the previous alienations of capitalism. To make man the master of his

history, to put in his hands power over the forces which endlessly escape him: this is doubtless an endless task that really deserves the name of permanent revolution.

But this is not all: new meanings of socialism have appeared through the very practice of socialist societies and derive much more from self-criticism of these societies than from the criticism of previous societies. There is the danger that socialism may not only reduce itself, as we have said, to the reign of administration and bureaucracy, but, more basically, that it may express the resumption under another form the project of bourgeois societies, to wit, a simple technique of well-being. Bourgeois society conceived capitalism itself as the means to achieve, through competition, the spirit of enterprise, risks and gambles, the fundamental objectives of an utilitarian ethics. Socialism could turn out only to be, by means of superior rationality and better technology, the resumption of the same hedonistic ethics; socialism would then only be a more advanced and more rational industrialism pursuing the same dream of the Promethean conquest of well-being and of nature. It would only have pursued in a more rational way mastery of the world by means of a society geared to total satisfaction.

This danger is not fictitious; we have been for a century witnessing the progressive decline of the great dream of the founders of socialism, which was to assign to labor the most fundamental meaning of human activity. Yet work appears more and more as the simple economic cost of leisure, while leisure, to the degree that it is overcome by the mass technology that insidiously degrades it, appears increasingly as a mere diversion and as a mere compensation for the sacrifice of working. We are perfectly able to foresee and even already to glimpse the danger in a society of consumption or of abundance in which socialism would be reduced to the ridiculous triumph of the socialization of the *ordinary man*. It is thus an essentially spiritual danger which awaits socialism at this level. It is this danger that is already at work in the welfare state and in Scandinavian socialism.

To face this danger, we must constantly go back to what is the least technical and the closest to the "heart" of Socialism: more deeply than a technique, socialism is the cry of distress, the demand and the hope of the most humbled men. This is why today one cannot separate socialism from solidarity with the most underpriviledged fraction of humanity, with the misery of the underdeveloped peoples. If the socialist aspiration is not fundamentally linked with the revolt of the slaves, it is no more than a rational and dehumanized calculation, the specter of which has not yet ceased haunting us. "As if," Péguy said, "the affairs of socialism never ceased to be the affairs of humanity." The weakness of the welfare state is the lack of a human perspective. The strength of the socialist camp is precisely the feeling of collective work being done. The friendship, irrespective of borders, for those who work and suffer and the deep feeling of belonging to a single humanity must not be lost. This is the role of utopia that I have discussed so many times in this journal. Without utopia, only calculation and technocracy remain. It is at this level of socialism's constant spiritual re-establishment that the true dialogue with Christianity must be instituted, maintained, and renewed.

13

ETHICS AND CULTURE
HABERMAS AND GADAMER IN DIALOGUE

T HE INTENTION OF THIS ESSAY IS TO CLARIFY THE CEN-
tral antinomy of moral philosophy by placing it
in relation to a similar antinomy which affects the
relations of a moral agent with his cultural heritage
or cultural heritages. Thus the title of the essay,
"Ethics and Culture," which designates the two foci
of an ellipse.

THE ANTINOMY OF VALUE

The central antinomy of moral philosophy, it seems
to me, concerns the status of the notion of *value*.

On the one hand, we oppose values to things in
order to bind them to freedom. Drawing the most
extreme consequences of the Kantian concept of
autonomy we say that values are the work of freedom,
that they express its power of innovation or renovation, its creative spontaneity. On the other hand, it

Translated by David Pellauer

243

does not seem that it depends upon our will that values outline a certain order, a certain hierarchy; for example, that respect for the other person should be superior to values of simple utility. It seems here that values can only orient action because they are discovered, not created. Without being things, they would then have the status of being an essence.

This dilemma is an authentic antinomy to the extent that some undeniable traits of our individual and collective experience seem to justify one or the other thesis in such a way that it seems as if we ought to accept them both without having caught sight of the mediations which render them compatible. On the one hand, experience seems to say that we most merit being called a moral agent when, confronted by a unique situation, we respond to its challenge with an equally unique decision, which is not justified by any precedent. Situational ethics makes this extreme case the paradigmatic case to the exclusion of other aspects of the moral life. The other face of the antinomy is illustrated by those forms of conduct whose morality results essentially from our willingness to obey the principle of truthfulness, or the rule of honor, or the duty of friendship, or from loyalty to the party. Truthfulness, in this instance, is the best touchstone, as we have known since Kant. For as flexible as a casuistry may make applications, this maxim does not appear to plead in principle for an invention of the rule in terms of the case, as a philosophy of the creation of values seems to require.

The ethical antinomy finds its highest expression, however, within the very figure of the creators of morality. On one side, attesting to the historical character of morality, these geniuses invent new manners of evaluation as witnessed to by their conduct and their teaching. An excellent example of such "transvaluation" is offered by the manner in which the maxim of vengeance was overcome by the rule of justice in the penal codes of the ancient Near East and in ancient Greece. But, from another point of view, wise men are the first to say that they do not invent anything, that they rather rediscover an ancient law, whether this forgotten law be that of nature, or of feeling, or of reason. Here is the most extreme antinomy: the only true creators, it seems, are those who are capable at the same time of re-activating the meaning of or the feeling for an *ordo amoris* which it is not ours to create.

This antinomy is perhaps insolvable at the level of an abstract axiology. But it can be clarified a bit if we compare it to a comparable dilemma in the philosophy of culture which has the advantage of offering the perspective of a practical and concrete mediation.

This dilemma is the one which strikes our behavior in relation to our cultural heritages. In introducing the notion of a heritage I am doubtlessly restricting the field of questions which can be posed about culture, but I thereby hope to concentrate our attention on one essential trait of culture, one among many to be sure, but one at least in no way accessory or accidental. I mean that every culture comes to us as a received heritage, therefore as transmitted and carried by a tradition.

Three words have been used here: heritage, transmission, and tradition. The first underlines the fact that culture is one modality of the replacement of human generations by one another, by instituting the continuity of an historical memory across the biological discontinuity of the generations. This heritage is, moreover, a transmission in the sense that the continuity of the generations is assured through institutions, whether formal as in teaching and education, or informal as in costume and usage. Language is the first of these institutions, above all because it is fixed through writing. Transmission is thereby assured by the "documents" of the culture—works of art and of discourse—offered to the interpretation of the following generations. The third term of the sequence—heritage, transmission, tradition—is the one which gives birth to all the contradictions, all the conflicts upon which our reflection is going to linger.

Tradition says more than transmission, which is a relatively neutral term, susceptible at its limit to a purely technical interpretation close to that of the notion of information. Among the most controversial connotations of the word "tradition" is the idea of a cultural content transmitted by a specific authority, the authority of the past. All at once the word "tradition" loses all neutrality. It is not limited to describing our dependence on the past as a fact, instead it accords a positive value to that dependence. It presumes the superiority of a certain teaching because it is old, or ancient, or even archaic. It is here that the debate really begins, for this authority can appear to us in turn as a form of violence exercised against our thinking, which prevents us from advancing to maturity of judgment, or as a means of assistance, as a necessary guide on the pathway from infancy to maturity.

I would like to elaborate in a systematic fashion the conflict underlying these negative or positive evaluations of tradition.

THE ANTINOMY OF TRADITION

I could have taken as my guide here the exemplary debate between the spirit of the Enlightenment and that of Romanticism at the end of the eighteenth century and the beginning of the nineteenth century. This debate presents in a nicely antinomous fashion the two terms of the dilemma. On the one hand, "reason" was defined by its power to uproot itself from "tradition," tradition called prejudice (*Vorurteil*). Reason was this very uprooting. In return, the authority of tradition could only appear as a fetter, captivity, violence. For the Englightenment, reason and tradition were antinomous. As Kant cried, "*Sapere Aude!*" In the face of the Enlightenment, Romanticism appeared as a simple reversal of pro and con. It magnified *mythos* where the Enlightenment had celebrated *logos*. It pleaded for the old at the expense of the new, for historic Christianity as opposed to the modern state, for fraternal community instead of a society of law, for unconscious genius rather than sterile consciousness, for poetic imagination, not cold ratiocination. But Romanticism did not know how to bring to light the necessary presuppositions for a critique of prejudice, namely the sovereignty of judgment, the universality of reason, and the condition of a free will without any historical encumbrance. This is why it was limited to reversing the

247

answer without reversing the question. So here the antinomy had not yet reached its true breadth.

The relative sterility of this debate leads me to look closer to our own day for a more accomplished, a more authentic, and a more dramatic form of the antinomy. I find this more complete form in the debate which in these past years has opposed hermeneutical philosophy stemming from Heidegger and represented in a remarkable fashion by Gadamer in his *Wahrheit und Methode*, and the critique of ideologies issuing from the Frankfurt School, and behind this from Marxism, as illustrated by Jürgen Habermas in *Erkenntnis und Interesse*. I want to extract from this controversy what might be of interest to our problem, namely the status of historical heritages, transmission, and tradition, as the locus of the emergence of values in history.

While hermeneutical philosophy sees in tradition a dimension of historical consciousness, an aspect of participation in cultural heritages and reactivation of them, the critique of ideologies sees in the same tradition the place par excellence of distortions and alienations and opposes to it the regulative idea, which it projects into the future, of communication without frontiers and without constraint.

This debate is exemplary to my eyes because it offers privileged access to the unsolved problem of the origin of values. In effect, the somewhat abstract idea of an order of values which is to be discovered takes on a concrete visage when it is placed within the framework of a mediation on historicity and the notions which follow from it: pre-understanding, prejudgment, and therefore also tradition and

authority. What is more, the equally abstract idea
of a creative freedom with regard to values also
takes on a sort of flesh when it is applied to the
critical enterprise of unmasking illusions and dismantling ideological systems which hold freedom
captive. Freedom is then no longer the free examination of the Enlightenment, but the liberation engendered by a real critique of the systematic distortions
of communication.

What really makes this debate exemplary, therefore, is its radicality. Instead of being content with
consequences or appearances—the authority of tradition, or the misleading nature of prejudices—both
philosophies dig down to the roots of the debate which,
finally, bring into the play the ultimate meaning
of the basic philosophical gesture. We are forced to
ask whether doing philosophy is to assume a condition of finitude for which historicity, pre-understanding, and prejudice are the implications, or if to
do philosophy is to say "no"—to criticize in the
strongest sense of the word, in the name of the future
of freedom, anticipated in a regulative idea.

Yet at the same time that the debate between hermeneutics and the critique of ideologies makes the
central antinomy of the philosophy of values more
concrete and more radical, it also discloses a mediation of a particular kind, let us say of a circular,
practical, and concrete relation, between the sort of
participation which is the soul of historical consciousness and the sort of distanciation which is the soul
of every critical philosophy. If the debate between
hermeneutics and the critique of ideologies can
therefore be less sterile than the one which I men-

tioned above between the Enlightenment and Romanticism, it may be seen to be capable of unravelling the initial antinomy of value whose terms I will recall once more. If values are not our work but precede us, why do they not suppress our freedom? And if they are our work why are they not arbitrary choices?

Our reflection will not be in vain if it allows us to replace this antinomy by a living circle.

HERMENEUTICS AND TRADITION

For a superficial reading of the writings in question, the opposition between hermeneutics and a critique of ideologies might appear just as futile as that which previously took place between the Enlightenment and Romanticism, for in various ways both philosophies repeat the thesis of the Enlightment and of Romanticism.

Hermeneutical philosophy, in effect, is not addressed directly to the ethical problem of values, any more than it is limited to the epistemological problem of the human sciences. It digs beneath both problems in such a way as to bring to light their roots. The basic experience around which *Wahrheit und Methode* is organized and from which hermeneutics raises up its claim to universality is that of the scandal which constitutes the sort of "alienating distanciation" (*Verfremdung*) which appears to it to be the presupposition of every human science. This alienating distanciation is more than a feeling or a mood. It is the ontological presupposition which underlies the objective conduct of the human sciences. The methodology of these sciences necessarily implies a taking of distance, which in its turn expresses the destruction of the primordial relation of participation —of *Zugehörigkeit*—without which there would not exist any relation to the historical as such.

This debate between alienating distanciation and the experience of participation is traced by Gadamer in the three spheres among which the hermeneutical experience is divided: the aesthetic sphere, the historical sphere, and the sphere of language. Within the aesthetic sphere, the experience of being grasped by a work of art always precedes and makes possible the critical exercise of judgment, for which Kant has given the theory in terms of the judgment of taste. Within the historical sphere, the consciousness of being carried by traditions which precede me is what makes possible every exercise of a historical methodology at the level of the human and the social sciences. Finally, within the sphere of language, which in a way overlaps the two preceding spheres, the co-belonging to things articulated by the great voices of creators of discourse precedes and makes possible every scientific treatment of language as an available instrument and every pretension to dominate the structures of the text of our culture by objective techniques.

We can understand that on the basis of this massive opposition between participation and distanciation a certain rehabilitation of prejudice, authority, and tradition becomes possible again: a human being discovers his finitude in the fact that, first of all, he finds himself within a tradition or traditions. Because history precedes me and my reflection, because I belong to history before I belong to myself, prejudgment also precedes judgment, and submission

251

to traditions precedes their examination. The regime of historical consciousness is that of a consciousness exposed to the effect of history. If therefore we cannot extract ourselves from historical becoming, or place ourselves at a distance from it in such a way that the past becomes an object for us, then we must confess that we are always situated within history in such a fashion that our consciousness never has the freedom to bring itself face to face with the past by an act of sovereign independence. It is rather a question of becoming conscious of the action which affects us and of accepting that the past which is a part of our experience keeps us from taking it totally in charge, of accepting in some way its truth.

Let us pause here. It is clear that if hermeneutics limits itself to this antithesis between distanciation and participation, it has only renewed the positions of Romantic philosophy against the Enlightenment without really rejuvenating them. I want to show later, however, after having also outlined the opposing thesis in a schematic manner, that hermeneutical philosophy has other resources and that it is required by its internal logic to reintroduce a *critical moment*—or as I will say more precisely later, a *critical distance* —as a necessary dialectical factor of the hermeneutical process. But we are not yet ready to show how a consciousness of belonging, expressly defined by the refusal of distanciation, can and must receive within itself a particular critical moment.

THE CRITIQUE OF IDEOLOGIES

It is time to introduce the second protagonist. Here, too, I will limit myself to those arguments likely to

contribute to the present discussion. The first movement of a philosophical critique of ideologies is the
placing of philosophical discourse in its entirety
under the aegis of a concept of interest, which proceeds directly from the Marxist critique of philosophical discourse in general and of Hegelian discourse
in particular. Philosophical hermeneutics is re-
proached for remaining in the widest sense of the word
a philosophy of discourse, even though it speaks of
aesthetics and history and even though it treats the
dimension of language as a simple place for the
articulation of our aesthetic and historical experience.
The initial vice of a philosophy of interpretation is
that it leaves out the most fundamental anthropological structure articulated in terms of the concepts
of work, power, and language. This preliminary extension of the anthropological sphere, according to
Habermas, echoes the great discovery which he credits
to Marx, namely, that the "synthesis of the object"
is incomplete in pure understanding and complete in
work. This is why, he says, that Marxism is, in relation to the Kantian critique, the first meta-critique.

This first step of the critique of ideologies cannot
fail to affect our debate centered on the axiological
problem. The problem of the origin of values is
perhaps insoluble as long as it is posed by a philosophy
which is conceived of as *theoria*. The solution may
be less inaccessible on the ground of *praxis*, though,
as the priority of the concept of interest over that of
knowledge suggests.

The second thesis which I want to retain from the
critique of ideologies brings us closer to this goal.
If it is the task of a meta-critique to unmask the

interests hidden behind every pretension to pure knowledge, it is also its task to resist every effort to reduce the sphere of interests to a single kind of interest. According to Habermas, three interests govern all human activity. Each one of them constitutes the transcendental condition for a certain sphere of meaning in that it determines the *a priori* conditions for the apprehension of a certain type of object and it commands a certain type of scientificity. Thus "instrumental interest" governs the whole world of empirical sciences. The "facts" capable of being apprehended at this level are carved out by our cognitive interest directed toward technical control as applied to objectified processes. As regards "practical" interest," also called "interest in communication," it governs the whole world of historical-hermeneutical sciences. The statements relevant to this sphere no longer just satisfy the criteria of predictability and exploitability, they draw their meaning from their capacity to promote the exchange of messages within ordinary discourse, the understanding of texts received from tradition, and the interiorization of norms which institutionalize social roles. It is at this level therefore that the historical sciences are hermeneutical sciences, that is, sciences of interpretation, necessarily placed under the regime of the hermeneutical circle. The understanding of significations under the jurisdiction of this plan is inseparable from the capacity of present historical agents to take up the significations of the past in a creative interpretation and thus to promote communication. This is why practical interest is also called "interest in communication."

I will not discuss here the question of whether the declared proximity of Heidegger and Gadamer is more apparent than real, or the question, at what point can Marxism be reinterpreted on the basis of such a division between instrumental and practical interest. The question remains open, to me, whether the phenomenon of domination and all the distortions which are attached to it does not suppose just as deep a distinction between communicative action and instrumental action.

It is with the third interest that we really enter into the heart of the debate. This third interest is called by Habermas the "interest in emancipation." With it we are at the heart of the problematic of values, at the source of the creative origin of values, for it appears that this interest also defines the highest value, namely, freedom as it grasps itself as a process of emancipation. It is true that it is not as the source of values that the author develops this concept, but as the transcendental condition of a third sort of science which we have not yet mentioned, the critical social sciences, whose introduction marks the most significant break with hermeneutical philosophy. The problem is no longer to reinterpret traditions by struggling against alienating distanciation, but to project our future autonomy as the very meaning which we give to every critical enterprise.

The introduction of the concept of ideology seals the break. What characterizes ideology is that it cannot be treated as a particular case of misunderstanding, amenable to interpretative methods which would dissolve it into a higher understanding. Ideology is first of all a distortion engendered at the same

255

level where work, power, and discourse are inter-
twined. As we have seen, this intertwining is not
recognized by hermeneutics as long as it remains
within the limits of a philosophy of discourse. Moreover, ideology is a distortion stemming from violence
and repression, comparable to the effects of censorship as described by Freudian psychoanalysis, with
the result that ideology is an effect of meaning for
which the subject lacks the key. In principle an ideology
is not aware of itself as an ideology. This unconscious
status of an ideology decides the kind of strategy
capable of being applied to it. It is no longer possible
to oppose "understanding" and "explanation" in the
fashion of Dilthey. Only properly explanatory procedures, once again comparable to those of psychoanalysis, are capable of leading to a reconstruction of what
would be in the theory of ideologies the equivalent
of the "primitive scene" in psychoanalytic theory.
In both cases the movement from "desymbolization"
to "resymbolization" takes place through the dissolution of a system of distortions which can in no way
be understood as an extension of the interpretative
method, that is, as a movement from misunderstanding
to understanding.

We can understand in what sense the third interest
in question here can be said to be "critical" by
nature. The interest in emancipation is only active
in the work of unmasking hidden systematic distortions. In return, this critique would be impossible if
the sort of interest which we are calling "interest
in emancipation" was not itself at work. In order to
say in what this interest consists, we must be content
to recognize it as having the status of a Kantian idea.

It is a regulative idea whose content is limited to requiring communication without any constraint or limit. This is to say that this interest is of the order of anticipation rather than one of reminiscence. An eschatology of non-violence, akin to Ernst Bloch's "principle of hope," is the ultimate horizon of this philosophy. At the same time, not only its critical but utopian turn seems to oppose this philosophy diametrically to a hermeneutical philosophy, which in contrast appears to renew the philosophies of reminiscence. The critical thinker does not speak as the poet does of "the dialogue which we are," but of the idea of communication which we are not, but which we ought to be.

In the critical reflections which follow and for which I alone am responsible, I would like to demonstrate two things. First, that a hermeneutic of traditions can only fulfill its program if it introduces a critical distance, conceived and practiced as an integral part of the hermeneutical process. And secondly, and on the other hand, that a critique of ideologies too can only fulfill its project if it incorporates a certain regeneration of the past, consequently, a reinterpretation of tradition. From these two arguments I will draw several consequences concerning the theory of values and, in general, the axiological problem.

PRODUCTIVE DISTANCIATION

It is within the very concept of historical efficacity, understood by Gadamer as consciousness exposed to the effects of history, that I discern the necessity to overcome the massive opposition between participation and alienating distanciation. The consciousness of historical efficacity, in effect, contains within itself the moment of distance. The history of effects is precisely what takes place under the condition of historical distance. Historical efficacity is efficacity at a distance, which makes the distant near. Without the tension between the self and the other, there is no historical consciousness. This dialectic of participation and distanciation is the key to the concept of a "fusion of horizons" within which is expressed the communication of the present with the past. If the condition of the finitude of historical knowledge excludes every overview, every final synthesis in a Hegelian manner, this finitude is not such that I am enclosed within one point of view. Where there is a situation, there is a horizon which may either be narrowed or expanded. This makes possible communication at a distance between two differently situated consciousnesses. Their intentions blend in the distant and open horizon. We do not live therefore within closed horizons or within a unique horizon. The tension between the self and the other, between the near and the far, is accomplished on the distant horizon.

But it is principally the linguisticality of historical experience which forces the reintroduction of distanciation within the very interior of participation. The universal linguisticality of human experience signifies precisely that my belonging to a tradition or to traditions takes place through the interpretation of signs, texts, and works, within which cultural heritages are inscribed and offered for our decipherment. Moreover, linguisticality only exercises its

mediating function when the interlocutors both ef-
face themselves before the things spoken of, which
in a way lead the dialogue. Now this reign of the
thing said—is it not most apparent when mediation
by language becomes mediation through the text? That
which makes us communicate at a distance is the
"issue of the text," (*la "chose du texte"*) which no
longer belongs either to its author or its reader.

Dilthey had already reflected upon the positive
role of the "objectification" of the expressions of
life in cultural signs which are detached from their
creator to become autonomous realities which unfold
in turn their own historical effects. Dilthey also
noted that fixation through writing and by all comparable procedures of the inscription of human discourse is the major cultural event which conditions
all transmission of cultural heritages and every constitution of a tradition. Writing, in effect, assures
the triple autonomy of the text which characterizes
it: autonomy with regard to the reader and his intentions; autonomy with regard to the initial situation of
the discourse and from every social-cultural conditioning affecting that situation; and autonomy with
regard to the initial hearer and the original audience.

Such is the distanciation which I will call productive
distanciation, which at least in civilizations which
possess writing, makes possible the transmission
of every past heritage. For what is true of the signification of a work of art or for discourse is equally
true for the signification of values created by moral
geniuses, or by specific communities, or by historical
cultures. Let us consider for a moment the value
of "nobility" so dear to Nietzsche and Max Scheler.

It is not difficult to relate its birth to the existence of a certain class, the nobility precisely, and to a certain literature: epic cycles, courtly literature, etc. But what makes this creation an acquired value is its elevation to the status of a "text," in the sense of the word which henceforth surpasses the case of literature. This value becomes autonomous in relation to the intentions of those who pronounced and professed it. It is inscribed in our cultural patrimony. But it is also important to emphasize that it becomes independent with regard to the social-cultural conditions of its production. Just as the signification of a text causes the suspension—the *Aufhebung*—of its historical-cultural conditioning, so a value becomes valuable beyond the historical-cultural circumstances of its birth. We are exposed to the effects of its history to the degree that it is uprooted from the causal chain which engendered it in time. At the same time, in freeing itself with regard to its initial audience, it is open to a whole series of reinterpretations which reactualize it each time in a new situation.

DISTANCIATION AND PARTICIPATION

This last remark concerning the possibility of re-activating an old value within a new situation leads me to my second series of critical remarks, applied this time to the critique of ideologies. I will note first that a theory of interest and of interests brings into play a philosophical anthropology very different in principle from the sort of abstract rationalism which had earlier motivated the Enlightenment, although it is true, as we will see later, that our considerations applied to the third interest, the interest in emancipation, strongly threaten to put the same abstract idealism back in business. But in principle the anthropology underlying the theory of interests expresses the same subordination of theory and knowledge to the profound movement of human existence as that which is expressed in the Heideggerian theory of care.

I willingly admit that the primacy accorded by Habermas to the concept of interest proceeds from a happy contamination between the Marxist concept of *praxis* and the Heideggerian concept of care much more than from any kinship with the concept of utility in the tradition of English utlitarianism or with the concepts of American pragmatism. Yet the most important aspect of the theory of interest is not its rootedness in an anthropology whose basic terms remain undetermined, but its recourse to a hierarchical principle. The distinction between an instrumental interest, a practical interest, and an interest in emancipation outlines a system of preferences which in turn appeals to a discernment of the rank of values which can hardly be conceived of as a creation, but which may be conceived of as the recognition of an order, which in its final sense is less distant from Max Scheler than it might appear to be. In brief, I do not see how anyone can construct a theory of interest and interests without the help of an anthropology and an axiology.

Someone may object, it is true, that this axiology escapes the alternatives of creation or intuition to the degree that each interest is in a way the result of a transcendental deduction (in the Kantian sense of the word) for a certain region of objects, for the epistemology corresponding to these objects, and finally for behaviors of every sort that are relative to this sphere. Thus, as we have seen, the instrumental interest opens a space of meaning within which facts in the empirical sense of the word may be apprehended, which are at the same time predictable, exploitable, and manipulable objects. It is the same for the sphere of practical interest still called interest in communication. Its justification proceeds from the transcendental function which it exercises with regard to the historical-hermeneutical sciences whose space of meaning is opened up by this specific interest. Finally, there is no need to repeat that the interest in emancipation is inseparable from the coming into play of the critical social sciences.

My quarrel, however, does not really bear on the notion of interest, nor on the principle of a hierarchization of interests. On the contrary, I take from the concept of interest an important warning which hermeneutical philosophy must heed—that the forgetfulness of the trilogy work-power-languages can always lead to a disastrous retreat into a philosophy of language which would lose its anthropological breadth. Hermeneutical philosophy must not only heed this warning, but also accept it. The very fact that linguisticality should be subordinated to historical experience and to aesthetic experience is sufficient warning that language is only the locus for the articulation of an experience which supports it, and that everything, consequently, does not arrive *in* language, but only comes *to* language. There is therefore no reason why work and power should not be taken into account in an anthropology of care where the linguistic dimension finds its privileged, yet subordinate place.

My quarrel, if there is a quarrel, concerns the possibility of giving a concrete content to the third interest, the interest in emancipation, without founding it upon the second interest, the practical interest or interest in communication.

First, how do we know that the interest in emancipation stands at the summit of the hierarchy of interests? Is it in virtue of the epistemological function which is attached to it, its capacity to found the critical social sciences? We could certainly affirm this, since this interest is the transcendental condition for a corresponding science. But why must there here be critical social sciences which are not just descriptive and explanatory sciences? The explicit epistemological function seems to be derived from an implicit axiological position, similar to the one which led Max Scheler to place the person at the summit and the heart of his ethics. A circular relation is thereby established between the axiological position and the epistemological function.

In itself, the recognition of a circular relation is in no way scandalous, if it is not from the same point of view that the axiological position and the epistemological function reciprocally justify themselves. Kant, for example, was in no way embarrassed to say that freedom was the *ratio essendi* of the law and the law the *ratio cognoscendi* of freedom. The interest in emancipation and the intelligiblity of the critical social sciences seem to be in a comparable relation. This said, my question is the following. Is it possible to distinguish and, even more so, to oppose the interest in emancipation and the practical interest still called interest in communication? Can the circle which the first constitutes with the critical social sciences really be dissociated from the circle which the second constitutes with the historical-hermeneutical sciences? Here is my point of doubt. I am inclined to emphasize the complementary character of these two orders of sciences and the two modalities of interests which govern the corresponding methodologies.

As regards, first, the respective methodologies of the historical-hermeneutical sciences and the critical social sciences, I am most suspicious of the old opposition between understanding, which would be the portion of the first science, and explanation, which would be the lot of the second. If the communication of past heritages takes place under the condition of distanciation and objectification, then explanation is a necessary step for understanding. We always explain in order to better understand. A text must be explained in its internal structure before being understood in its relation to the interest it arouses and to which it responds. It is no different for a value or for a group of values which have become an enduring cultural acquisition. But the opposite is just as true. If understanding passes through explanation, explanation is completed in understanding. This rule is just as valid for the explanation of ideologies and the systematic distortions which affect our competence to communicate. It is correct to say that these systematic distortions call for a genetic explanation. But genetic explanation remains rightly insignificant—"senseless" in the strongest sense of the word—if it is not meant to re-establish a larger field of consciousness, and to restore this same competence to communicate which had deteriorated. Explanation only makes sense if it is interpolated with a "desymbolization" and a "resymbolization," both of which concern our capacity to communicate with others and to understand ourselves.

Thus the two methodologies refer to each other and it therefore seems useless to me to oppose the problematic of ideology to that of misunderstanding, which hermeneutics sensibly combats. The ideological phenomenon is only provisionally irreducible to prejudice or prejudgment, which hermeneutics makes an aspect of pre-understanding, that is, of our finite condition and our irreducible perspective due to our belonging to history. To reduce an ideological process is first undoubtedly to explain it, but in such a way that the pre-understanding we have of our situation and our project becomes less opaque and more transparent. We could only completely detach the explanation of ideologies from the movement by which we clarify the preliminary understanding which we have of ourselves if a non-historical place existed, one not situated historically, from where we could consider from a distance and from on high the theater of illusions, the battle field of ideologies. Then it would be possible to explain without understanding. But this explanation would no longer have anything to do with the restoration of our competence to communicate and therefore with the emancipation of the human species.

Therefore it is to the level of interests themselves and not only to the level of the methodology of the corresponding sciences for which these interests open the space of meaning that we must carry the discussion.

My thesis here is that the interest in emancipation would be empty and anemic unless it received a concrete content from our practical interest in communication and, therefore, if it were not confirmed by our capacity to creatively reinterpret our cultural heritages.

What encourages me to tie the projection of our interest in emancipation so closely to the reinterpretation of the tradition of the past are the conclusions drawn from the analysis of industrial societies advanced by the theory of ideologies, at least as it has been adopted by several thinkers stemming from the Frankfurt School or close to it, such as Marcuse in the United States and Jacques Ellul in France. For these thinkers, it is science and technology which tend today to assume the ideological function earlier exercised by religion. This new ideology is asked to justify the perpetuation of the industrial system, become an end in itself, or rather to deploy itself as a dynamic of means without any end. We can call this function of signification ideological to the degree that it tends to conceal the disfunctions of our social life in the name of the preservation of the industrial system and its expansion. As in the case of past ideologies, this functioning escapes the consciousness of individuals and groups and develops a whole set of repressive measures with regard to anything that might call into question, either theoretically or practically, the perpetuation of the system. The occurrence of modern ideology in the delicate interplay of interests is easy to recognize: the hierarchy of interests tends to be crushed, to be reduced to the level of a single instrumental interest. This is how today we witness the industrialization and the manipulation of our whole cultural life.

But if such is the case, I ask, how is it still possible to combat this reduction to a unidimensionality in the order of interests and values? How is it still possible to preserve the difference between the "good life" constantly professed by philosophers and the purely quantitative growth of material goods which appears to be the sole law of the industrial system? It seems to me that only the conjunction between the critique of ideologies, animated by our interests in emancipation, and the reinterpretation of the heritages of the past, animated by our interest in communication, may yet give a concrete content to this effort. A simple critique of distortions is just the reverse side and the other half of an effort to regenerate communicative action in its full capacity. If we had no experience whatsoever of an effective communication—even if this comes from the narrow sphere of interpersonal relations—the regulative idea of communication without frontiers and without constraint would remain a kind of wishful thinking, if not an outburst of schizophrenic demands in modern society.

A "PRACTICAL" SOLUTION TO THE ANTINOMY OF VALUES

Allow me to draw from this debate between a hermeneutic of traditions and a critique of ideologies some conclusions concerning the axiological problem which introduced our investigation.

First, the antinomy which appears to us to characterize this problem finds its confirmation in a similar antinomy at the level of the cultural conditions of axiology. On the one hand, none of us finds himself placed in the radical position of creating the ethical world *ex nihilo*. It is an inescapable aspect of our finite condition that we are born into a world already qualified in an ethical manner by the decisions of our predecessors, by the living culture which Hegel called the ethical substance, and by the reflection of wise and experienced men. In brief, we are always already preceded by evaluations beginning from which even our doubt and our contestation become possible. We can perhaps "transvaluate" values, but we can never create them beginning from zero. The passage through tradition has no other justification than this antecedence of the ethical world with regard to every ethical subject.

But, on the other hand, we never receive values as we find things or as we find ourselves existing in a world of phenomena. It is only under the aegis of our interest in emancipation that we are stirred to transvaluate what has already been evaluated. It is this interest in emancipation which introduces what I call "ethical distance" in our relation to any heritage. For the philosopher at least, ethical naïveté has been lost, Hegel's beautiful substance is blemished. Nothing survives from the past except through a reinterpretation in the present which takes hold of the objectification and the distanciation which have elevated previously living values to the rank of a text. Ethical distance thus becomes a productive distance, a positive factor in reinterpretation.

Our detour through the theory of culture has not only confirmed the antinomy of the theory of values, it has also allowed us to catch sight of the process of mediation by which this antinomy is ceaselessly overcome. There are no other paths, in effect, for carrying out our interest in emancipation than by incarnating it within cultural acquisitions. Freedom only posits itself by transvaluating what has already been evaluated. The ethical life is a perpetual transaction between the project of freedom and its ethical situation outlined by the given world of institutions.

If we break this living circle somewhere, the self-positing of freedom is condemned to remain either an empty concept or a fanatical demand, even if we announce our interest in emancipation in a new language. Freedom remains an empty concept as long as it is limited to reaffirming the idealistic concept of a self-reflection which the theory of interest should have rendered impossible. And freedom is a fanatical concept as long as it simply remains the negation of every mediation. In this regard the Hegelian critique of empty freedom in chapter six of *The Phenomenology of Mind* on "Terror" ought to stand as a warning to every philosophy which would define itself in simple utopian terms.

However, on its side, a hermeneutic which would cut itself off from the regulative idea of emancipation would be no more than a hermeneutic of traditions and in these terms a form of philosophical restoration. Nostalgia for the past would drive it unpityingly toward the positions of Romanticism which it had started out to surpass.

The exchanges which we have tried to describe between explanation and understanding, between a critique of ideologies and the extension of communication, between the projection of freedom and the reinterpretation of the heritages of the past, outline the concrete mediation which axiology demands.

This mediation is a practical mediation. Without a doubt there is no theoretical solution to the fundamental antinomy of axiology. Only the work of evaluation—which is also a work of transvaluation—assures us that the relation between the project of freedom and the memory of its past conquests constitutes a vicious circle only for analytic understanding, not for practical reason.

14

The Tasks of the Political Educator

I PRESUPPOSE THAT I AM ADDRESSING MEN AND WOMEN who neither consider themselves disengaged intellectuals nor militants subject to party discipline. I presuppose that I am addressing intellectuals who are looking for ways they can honestly exercise effective action as political educators. I say at once that I place in this extremely vast category all those who feel responsible for the transformation, the evolution, and the revolution of their countries by an act of thought, of speech and of writing. These men, moreover, are found in unions, parties, cultural groups and in churches. It is at this level of responsibility that I will constantly try to confine myself.

My exposition will call for two parts: in the first, I will try to determine at what level of society we, as political educators, can be effective; in the second, I will try to determine the broad outlines of this effectiveness.

Translated by David Stewart

ANALYSIS OF THE PHENOMENON OF CIVILIZATION

Before undertaking the description of the phenomenon of civilization, I should point out at once what
my method is going to be: it will be essentially
analytic. I mean by this that I will proceed by means
of a series of divisions only provisionally determining
a series of levels and articulating these levels. I will
explain in due time the usefulness of this method.

One more remark: I take the word "civilization"
in its larger sense which covers three realities—
industries,[1] institutions, and values. This is to say
that I will not engage in the debate—as academic
as sterile—on "civilization and culture." This debate is linked to the different origin of words. In
German sociology, the word *Kultur* tends to take
on a restricted sense which covers only the third
reality—the exercise of values—whereas the word
Civilization has very rapidly taken on a much broader
meaning which covers the three realities already
mentioned. But one also speaks of acculturation in
order to indicate the growth of civilization in all its
aspects. There is therefore no reason to linger over
this debate.

I will speak at first on the level of industries. I
mean by this a very vast aspect of civilization which
goes beyond the level of tools, machines, and even
of techniques. An industry is everything which can
be considered as the accumulation of experience.
Certainly it is with the tool and the machine that
one understands best what industry signifies. Conservation is the first phenomenon to consider; by
conservation the tool survives its occasional use.
Innovation can be applied to the tool thus conserved,

and a wholly particular historical character is thus attached to the accumulation of tools. This historical character consists in the fact that every invention, appearing in a historical time and space, is acquired for all men—with a more or less great delay, to be sure—but according to an unchallengeable universal destination. The production and accumulation of tools neither admits of any national character nor is it tied to a particular culture. It characterizes at the outset a universal acquisition for the benefit of the community of men.

But this mode of acquisition that one observes at best on the level of tools and machines characterizes more and more every aspect of our life, to the extent that tools and machines can be considered from the angle of the accumulation of experience. One could say, in a very general way, that industry concerns the collection of the means and mediations which allow a human collectivity to create new goods. Thus knowledge and the sciences, to the extent that we are not considering them only as real inventions but as collective experience, can be considered as an industry crystallized into disposable goods. It is this notion of "disposable goods" which permits me to characterize this first strategic level of civilization.

To broaden this description more, every human experience to the extent that it leaves traces—documents, monuments—is developed after the manner of an available industry. Intellectual, moral and spiritual experiences are accumulated under the form of works, visible monuments, books and libraries, which comprise the experience of humanity.

Seen from this angle, civilization is unique. Every invention is by right acquired for all men. Technological history of the human race is that of humanity considered as a single man, this single man of whom Pascal said "ceaselessly he learns and remembers." In this sense civilization is in the singular: there is *a* civilization; there is *the* civilization.

This unique and universal aspect of civilization has always existed, but it is only now that we can become vividly conscious of it. We are doubtless the first historical epoch to include as a dominant fact the consciousness of belonging to a single global civilization, to experience ourselves as a single humanity which enlarges its capital, its instruments and means of working, living and thinking. This single humanity, which is developing a single global civilization, experiences itself as a single historical subject which adds to his knowledge and power. One could even say that spiritual experience appears to this unique history as it is crystallized in durable cultural evidences which are accumulated after the manner of an industry. Such is the first level.

The second level is that of *institutions*. The first reading which we have made of our existence remains, in effect, abstract in the sense that civilization defined as the collection of available means at a given historical moment does not exist anywhere, one could say, in a bare and brute state. Each historical group only appropriates its own technical and economic reality through institutions. But in bringing in the phenomenon of the institution, we are making evident at the same time the plurality of historical experiences. The word "civilization" now ought to be taken in the plural: there are *several* civilizations in the sense that the whole of institutional forms in which humanity pursues its experience seems to be, as far as we can point out in time, first a historical multiplicity. The style of this history is that of a finite experience. Humanity only realizes its consciousness through closed figures, which are those of multiple institutional systems which regulate its historical experience. Each civilization, taken in this sense, discloses historical 'and geographical limits. Each has its area, its outlines, its vital centers, its radiating nuclei, its zones of influence. Each has a time, "makes its time," carves in history a period that it marks with its seal.

What do we mean here by institutions? Two things, it seems to me. First, the forms of social existence in which the relations between men are regulated in normative fashion. Rights are the most abstract expression of it. Under this first aspect—that of the forms of social existence—we define the statics of society. These statics are engendered by institutional confusion and codified in the extraordinary complexity of rights (constitutional rights, public rights, civil rights, penal rights, commerical rights, social rights, etc.). But the notion of the institution covers a much vaster field of experience than the judicial system of a given society. If we now consider institutions from the angle of social dynamics, the institution is no longer represented by rights but what we could call, in the broader sense of the word, politics—that is to say, the exercise of decision-making and force at the level of the community.

Here I am able to justify the analytic method that I practice. The articulation of the phenomenon of civilization on separate levels alone allows for the appearance of what is irreducible in politics in relation to economics and techniques. As long as we consider the industry of a civilization separately, we completely bracket the fundamental fact of the exercise of power. It is only when we uniquely take into consideration the power of decision-making of the community taken as a body, as a whole endowed with a central power, that we can make stand out what is original in the political phenomenon. The discussion of Marxism that I will offer presently will make the importance of this distinction readily apparent. It appears necessary to me to have at the outset a really clear view of the distinction between economics, which regulates the group of relations with respect to work and goods, and what we could call the history of power, which not only does not pose the same problems but neither arouses the same maladies nor exhibits the same pathology and, consequently, is not relieved by the same therapeutic. One can conceive of a regime which proposes to correct economic and social injustices but which itself represents a pathological phenomenon in the political order. This was the case with Stalinism in contemporary history. Therefore it is indeed necessary to distinguish between the two strategic levels —techniques and economics on the one hand, politics on the other hand. What appears to me to be central on the second level is the role of the political decision and the exercise of force by the public power. It is there that institutional dynamics are to be distinguished not only from the statics of industry but even from the dynamics of the first level. The principle of this dynamic was that of invention and innovation, which are tied to the development of knowledge and of scientific skill. We are therefore here on the plane of the free creation, whereas institutional dynamics are tied to power structures entirely determined and irreducible to any others.

At the same time, this second level requires categories entirely particular and irreducible to those which we have been able to consider at the first level—such as the notions of industry, accumulation, and progress. It is now necessary to make industry correspond to the notion of the institution, accumulation to decision-making, and progress to ambiguity, meaning by this that nothing is acquired in the institutional order. Historical experience teaches us that power has an ascension and a decline, that there is a birth and death of empires. Politics, therefore, does not exemplify the same process of accumulation which characterizes industry. Political experience is never an acquired experience; both progression and regression are possible. The same pretensions, the same illusions, the same faults can be repeated at different moments of history. Indeed a historical experience allows for the possiblity of decline or decadence. There is even a sociology of decadence, which is as essential as that of ascension or that of progression.

Here we are in an order where the exercise of power includes events. These are not events in the

277

order of industry. We can indeed consider a discovery as an event, but it only becomes a technological phenomenon when it is inscribed in the
development of an industry in order to mark its
growth. In this regard, the temporal structure of
accumulation is radically different from the historical experience of power, which allows for events
set in motion by persons, eventually by important
and great men of note. To the accumulation of capital
corresponds the "crisis," in the double sense of
conflict and decision-making. The order of the
crisis is that of fundamentally historical contingency.
This is why I have spoken here of ambiguity in opposition to progress. There is progress in the order
of industry in the widest sense one can give this
word which not only includes material techniques but
also intellectual and spiritual attainments. But what
men do through their institutions is always uncertain.
History—as history of power—is uncertain. It is
the collection of chances and perils, the possiblity
of gaining everything or losing everything. As a matter
of fact, the very notions of danger and salvation only
begin to take on meaning at this level.

Let us consider now the third level, that of *values*,
which point up a third reading, a third division in
the global phenomenon of civilization. What can one
understand by that? It is not necessary to take the
word "value" in an abstract and, if I dare say it,
too philosophical a sense. I mean by this that the
reflection of the moralist on values represents a
second level of systematization which presupposes
a common experience of values in a given community.
When I speak of values I am not therefore thinking of

abstraction elaborated by philosophical reflection, such as the notions of justice, equality, etc; still less, solemn essences inscribed in an intelligible heaven. I want to speak of concrete valorizations such as could be apprehended in the attitudes of men in regard to other men—in work, property, power, temporal experience, etc. Concerning this last point, the times of an industrial society certainly do not have the same significance and are not valorized in the same fashion as the times of an agricultural society.

In order to better point out the extremely concrete character of this notion of value, I will take up again the analysis of industry in order to point out that it is the industry which is abstract and value which is concrete, contrary to what one could think. An available tool remains an abstraction independently of the value that we give it and which inserts it in a historical context. An industry is only useful and only operates if it is appreciated and positively valorized. I will simply recall two ready examples. In *Tristes Tropiques*, Claude Levi-Strauss wrote of civilizations where the tools provided by the colonizer were not utilized because there was no category to apprehend them. One even sees tribes wither away near an industry because this industry cannot be integrated into the collection of values which vitally constitute this group. The same experience on another level was made by Greek society, which was able to develop an industry based on the invention of the techniques of geometry and nascent physics. But this industry was never systematically developed because the project of saving human labor in an epoch of slavery did not in itself constitute a positive value. It was only when it was asked how human effort could be spared that the idea of replacing slavery with the machine became itself a positive value. It does not suffice to say that ancient society did not develop its techniques because it had slaves; the inverse proposition is also important. It is because one has neither tested as a value that idea of saving human labor nor has considered as a value the growth of technical capital available for society that one is content with servile work.

It is always through evaluations and valorizations that the means become operative. In contrast, we live in societies which appreciate their industries and which even consider as a positive value the existence of developing socities which are constantly improving their standard of living. Thus we live under a new temporal regime which is no longer defined by stability but by continual growth.

What we are therefore calling values is the very substance of the life of a people. This is found expressed in practical mores which represent some sort of inertia, the statics of values. Under this thin skin of practical mores we find traditions, which are like the living memory of a civilization. Finally, at a deeper level we find what is perhaps the very kernel of the phenomenon of civilization—namely, a collection of images and symbols by which a human group expresses its adaptation to reality, to other groups, and to history. By images and symbols I mean those entirely concrete representations by which a group represents its own existence and its own values. One could speak in this sense of the ethico-mythical kernel, the kernel both moral and imaginative which embodies the ultimate creaturely power of a group. It is at this level of profundity that the diversity of civilization is most profound. One could say that each historical group has a concrete idea of its own existence which represents the settled form of its choice of existence. Each historical group in this sense has an *ethos*, an ethical singularity which is a power of creation linked to a tradition, to a memory, to an archaic rooting. It is doubtless here that we reach the concrete heart of civilization, whereas the available industry only represents the collection of abstract mediations of the group's existence. It is only by the collection of concrete attitudes, shaped by the valorizing imagination, that the human phenomenon historically realizes itself.

We touch here on what is most mysterious in the historical existence of man. Nowhere, in fact, can we discover a universal *ethos*, whereas on the first level we were able to discern the progression toward a universal technical civilization. Already, on the second level, we have recognized the fragmentary character of the experience of power. In burying ourselves in the ethical experience, we arrive at what one could call the experience of historical finitude, since humanity has played out its destiny in a diversity of languages, a diversity of moral experiences, and a diversity of spiritualities and religions. Humanity is here irreducibly plural.

Certainly, these grains of creativity—if one can put it this way—that represent each of the historical civilizations do not give rise to experiences radically shut off from one another. The experience which we have of the diversity of languages attests that if languages are multifarious, they can at least communicate. I emphasize the word "communicate." If we discover a strange language, we wager that it can be translated. Certainly one cannot translate everything, but at least there is no language which cannot be paralleled by another language, which cannot find in another language equivalences of meaning. This partial possiblity of translating certifies that humanity, in its depth, is one. Although this unity itself cannot be apprehended, one can only become conscious of it by means of communication and not by a process of identification and leveling. Whereas on the technical level men can become identical with one another, on the deeper level of historical creation, diverse civilizations can only communicate with each other according to the model of the translation of one language into another. And everyone knows how laborious the work of translation is. We are here on the level where the conquest of human unity is a painful experience.

As is evident, I have deliberately taken an analytic point of view toward the phenomenon of civilization and have refrained from any systematic view which would tie these three levels together. We do not have, it seems to me, the instrument of thought for apprehending the totality of the phenomenon. It is not that we have no idea or feeling of this totality; on the contrary, we feel our historical experience as a totalization in process. But all totalizations we attempt to name or designate are already premature syntheses, already violent syntheses. In this regard, I think that Marxism can be a very good tool of analysis—

but a dangeous tool when it is taken as a theory of totality. Every theory of totality is too limited and deadly to the extent that it can only do justice fully to what is irreducible in the political phenomenon (with reference to the technical and economic level) and—what is also irreducible—to the spiritual phenomenon (with reference to the political phenomenon). Consequently, the synthesis which we are able to apprehend ought to be considered a working hypothesis allowing for collective thinking on the three levels we have distinguished, but it should not hinder the free reading of the diversity of our historical experience. This is why I have placed the emphasis on the difference between these levels and their irreducibility rather on an eventual dialectic of these diverse levels.

LINES OF EFFECTIVENESS

I now want to say a few words about the action proper to the political educator and relate it to the three levels that we have proceeded to distinguish. We will adhere to them henceforth on the level of strategic intervention.

It would be a clumsy error to believe that the action of the political educator remains confined to the third level, that of values. That would be the mortal illusion of a disengaged, disincarnated, intellectual conception. Against this I want to protest strongly. What I want rather to show is that there is on each of the three levels a specific type of intervention which can be reduced neither to that of the technocrat on the first level, to that of the professional politican on the second level, nor to that of the writer, professor or the cleric on the third level.

What is therefore the task and the responsibility of the educator at the *level of industries*? The new fact that characterizes our contemporary society is that of available industries made the object of an economic plan, and the fact that we are nevertheless responsible for the systematic growth of these industries. By that we want to underscore not only the rational character of the economic plan but the appearance of a new human structure—that of collective choice. Man determines himself collectively as an active subject of his destiny. It is this notion of collective choice that, it seems to me, ought to be underscored at this level of intervention. The educator, especially in developed industrial societies, will no longer simply be a protestor (as he has been and as he still ought to be) faced with injustice and inequality, old forms of poverty and new forms created by industrialized economics; he ought also to prepare men for this responsibility of collective decision. Up to now we have thought of choice, and freedom more especially, as individual activities. We have too frequently identified freedom with that of the head of the corporation elaborating his manpower projection on the basis of the profit principle. This freedom for individual initiative was contemporaneous with an incoherent economics and a collection of economic misfortunes of which the mechanisms were misunderstood and unmastered. But we must learn how to conduct ourselves in a world which will be more and more the theater of decisions made on the collective scale. The task of the educator, then, appears twofold: first he should make apparent the ethical significance of every choice appearing to be purely economic. Secondly, he ought to struggle for the erection of a democratic economy.

The ethical significance of every economic choice: the more in fact an economy is an economy of projection, the more it extends the field of responsibility. Contrary to a completely erroneous image according to which the economic plan denotes the progress of the mechanization of human life, I think, on the contrary, that the development of a rational economy represents a conquest of decision over chance and fate. This is why it is important for the political educator to make apparent all the moral implications of a collective choice. Every planned economy, whether it is a question of the authoritarian plans of the Soviet Union and popular democracies, or the much more flexible plans of the French type, sets in motion a hierarchy of options loaded with human significance. It is a question each time of giving consumption, leisure, exhibitions of prestige and power, and culture their respective place and relative urgency. What do we finally want? An economy of consumerism? Or power? Or prestige? Or is it necessary to sacrifice the consumption and enjoyment of one or two generations to some later virtue? What do we want through this choice? What kind of man are we making? That is the question. More and more it will be the task of the political educator of modern times to initiate the citizen continually to the exercise of collective choice.

But at the very time we are confronted with the task of becoming conscious, we have to struggle for the building of a democratic economy. The only way, in fact, of compensating for the displacements of liberty from the sector of individual initiative to the sector of collective decisions is to allow for the participation in discussion and decision of the greatest possible number of individuals. That is the problem of democratic economics: how to make sure that collective choice is not confiscated by a small number—whether it be the party machine, technocrats, or pressure groups. This problem of the democratic economy will be the great problem of decades to come for, actually, it exists nowhere. We are only just now understanding the savage forms of economic planning. Here rigidity of authoritarian plans; there the coalition of private interests—hidden under the appearance of the public interest—everywhere, bureaucracy. The struggle that the Yugoslavs have conducted against bureaucracy appears quite significant to me: how can the collective choice be truly the choice of each, the choice of all? We are thus starting to recover, on the economic and social level, the problem which was that of the great English political thinkers since Locke—and in France with Rousseau—the problem of the social contract. How can the decision of each individual be made to support the decision of all? How can the general will be made the will of each? The people of the 18th century posed this problem as that of the birth of civil society. Today we are living at the birth of economic society.

Thus the political educator, by being inserted into this construction, defines a plan of strategic intervention, which makes him indeed not only the man of values but also the man of industry, in the sense that every question of industry is a question of choice, and every question of choice is finally a moral question. I will sum up this first point by saying that if the current development of our societies is the result of a collective creation, this calls for a collective responsibility. We therefore have to create the instruments of this collective responsibility. This is what I call democratic economics.

On the second, properly *political* level is offered to us the occasion of stating precisely the relationships between ethics and politics—relations, as one knows, that are difficult and full of snares. I want to say at once that I adopt as a working hypothesis, and I add as a personal guideline, a most fruitful distinction which I borrow from the great German sociologist of the beginning of this century, Max Weber. In his celebrated essay entitled *Politics as a Vocation* he distinguishes two levels of ethics, that which he calls the ethic of conviction and, on the other hand, the ethic of responsibility. It is useful to know that in his manuscripts Max Weber first wrote "ethic of power" for the latter. This preciseness is very important for what follows, for I am convinced, in fact, that the health of a collectivity rests ultimately on the justness of the relation between these two ethics. On the one hand the ethic of conviction is supported by cultural and intellecutal groups and by confessing communities, including the churches, which find here—and not at all in politics proper—their true point of insertion. On the other hand, the ethic of responsibility is also the ethic of force, of methodological violence, of calculated culpability. The task of the educator is, in my sense, that of maintaining a lively tension at this point. For if we reduce the ethic of conviction to the ethic of responsibility, we will sink to political realism and Machiavellism, which results from the constant confusion of means and ends. But on the other hand, if the ethic of conviction pretends to a kind of direct action, we will sink to all the illusions of moralism and clericalism. The ethic of conviction can only operate indirectly by the constant pressure which it exerts on the ethic of responsibility and power. The difference is that it is not tied to the possible and the reasonable but to what one could call the humanly desirable, the optimum ethic. If we take this ethic in its highest degree—as it is expressed in the Sermon on the Mount—it is readily apparent that the problem is not that of realizing this ethic immediately but that of expressing it indirectly by the group of pressures which it can bring to· bear on the ethic of responsibility. Moreover, the morality of innocence is not the only flaw in this direct intervention of the ethic of conviction. I think that clericalism is one of the aspects of this direct intervention of the religious community in political action by the mediation of parties, unions, or para-ecclesiastical groupings which play on the confusion of the two ethics. I think that the Christian in particular ought to practice the dual affiliation of, on the one hand, adherence to the ecclesial community—a medium of convictions—but on the other hand to join himself with other men on the level of responsibility, which is also that of force,

and exercise with them an action which can only be
a lay action.

I will give an example of this pressure of the ethic
of conviction on the ethic of responsibility—that of
utopia. I believe, in fact, that there is a historic
function of utopia in the social order. Only utopia
can give to economic, social, and political action a
human intention and, in my sense, a double intention: on the one hand the will of humanity as a totality;
on the other hand, the will of the person as a singularity. This is the reason I have just now allowed
the action of an indeterminate totality. In fact, it
includes part of the fundamental intention that each
historical experience cannot totally exhaust; there
is a universal ethic as I have said. Some years ago
in the unpublished debate of the Mutualité[2] on the
problem of the Marxist ethic (concerning whether or
not humanity could project its existence as an indivisible whole), this function of utopia was found to be
irreducible to any kind of scientific analysis. If
it is true that a social class, because it has been
crushed, is more sensitized to these universal values,
utopia is not, properly speaking, the possession of
each constituted group. It is this intention of a
humanity—taken as a single suffering and willing
being—that is the horizon of all our debates on inequality in the world, on the atomic menace, on
decolonization, or on what Francois Perroux[3] calls
the generalized economy.

But we cannot simply profess the utopia of a total
humanity. It is necessary for us at the same time
to profess that of the perfectly singularized, individual

realization of the human vocation. This second aspect becomes particularly evident in the face of the anonymity and dehumanization of the relations between individuals in the midst of industrial society. The barbaric forms of urbanism in which we are plunged, the leveling of tastes and talents by the techniques of consumption and leisure, indicate to us sufficiently that it is necessary to struggle on two fronts: on the one hand to gather humanity together, which is always threatened with being polarized into rival groups; on the other hand to save each person from the anonymity in which he sinks in modern civilization. This is why it is necessary to us to recapture afresh the word of Emmanuel Mounier[4] when he spoke of the personalist revolution and communal life. But one ought never to separate the one term from the other, for . communal life alone brings us back again toward the totalitarian peril, and the personal by itself brings us back again to the illusion of individualism.

A utopian thesis, it is necessary to repeat, does not have an effectiveness of its own; it has such only to the extent that it transforms step by step the historical experience that we are able to make on the level of institutions and on the level of industries. This is why utopia becomes falsehood when it is not articulated correctly concerning the possibilities offered to each epoch. For example, we all feel that equality alone is true. We are indeed convinced that men are fundamentally alike, that they lack innate distinctions, that each is the inheritor of the work of all, and that too great a difference between the levels of life debases human relationships. But we well know, on the other hand, that the egalitarian society cannot be immediately realized but only a progressive reduction of the differences between the levels and manners of life. One can well see it in socialist democracies; the scarcity of higher technicians causes the great variations in remuneration to remain inevitable, and egalitarian society can only be realized by a constant corrective action that I have called the pressure of the ethic of conviction on the ethic of responsibility.

On the third level there is also much to say. I will restrict myself to proposing to you two ideas. It seems to me at first that the major task of the educator is to integrate the universal technical civilization with the cultural personality, such as I have defined it above, with the historical singularity of each human group. In fact, the consumer society towards which we are advancing in the course of this century has a profoundly ambiguous significance. On the one hand, it undoubtedly represents progress —a better living for the masses who have access to basic goods. For the first time it is no longer by procurement for the benefit of a limited elite that humanity lives its destiny. It is on the very level of the masses that the power of making history is today experienced. But at the same time, this universal civilization exercises on the creative nucleus of each of the historical groups an eroding action and a subtle destruction. Nevertheless, for each of the historical societies, the developing as well as those advanced in industrialization, the task is to exercise a kind of permanent arbitration between technical universalism and the personality constituted on the

ethico-political plane. All the struggles of decolonization and liberation are marked by the double necessity
of entering into the global technical society and being
rooted in the cultural past.

A balance ought to be induced on the level where
the different temporalities meet—the times of acquisition and progress, the times of creation and
memory. The technological world in itself is without
a past. Each invention erases the preceding, and we
are hurled into a sort of futurism. And yet we truly
have personality—individual and cultural—only to
the extent that we entirely assume our past, its values
and its symbols, and are capable of reinterpreting
it totally. This arbitration between many temporalities
constitutes the great problem of culture.

This problem does not concern advanced industrial
societies less than developing societies. They are
also threatened with losing their meaning in the
exercise of pure technology. To the extent that a
consumer society is developed, we still experience
more vividly the contradiction between the growing
rationality of our means and the disappearing rationality of our ends.

This first task calls for a second: all the values
of the past cannot survive; only those can which are
susceptible to what I have come to call reinterpretation. Thus only the spiritualities can survive which
take into account the responsibility of man, which
give meaning to material existence, to the technical
world, and in a general fashion to history. The dualistic spiritualities of evasion ought to die. In this regard,
Christianity ought to see through to the end the
crisis which will settle its two orientations—that

which turns toward Platonism and the contemplative experience and caused Nietzsche to say that it was only a Platonism for the people, and that which turns toward history, the incarnation, and the realization of brotherhood between men. Most generally, I think that the forms of spirituality which cannot take into account the historical dimension of man ought to succumb to the pressure of technical civilization. But on the other hand, I think that only a return to the past and a living reinterpretation of tradition can permit modern societies to resist the leveling to which the consumer society submits. We are touching here on the work of culture, more precisely, on the work of language, which our criticism of the idea of civilization entrusts to the hermeneutic problem.

But I will not be willing for anyone to dissociate the three tasks we have assigned to the political educator and which correspond to the three levels of intervention of the political educator. The struggle for a democratic economy offers a project both for the collection of men and for the single person —the reinterpretation of the traditional past facing the ascent of consumer society.

NOTES

1.   "Industries" translates *outillages*, which Ricoeur juxtaposes with *outils*, translated throughout as "tools." *Tr.*

2.   Mutualité is a meeting hall in Paris owned by the French Communist Party. *Tr.*

3.   Professor of economics at the College de France. Among his many published works are *Le Capitalisme* (6th ed., 1965), *La Coexistence pacifique*, 2 vols (1958), and *L'Enterprise et l'economie de XXe siecle* (3 vols, 1966-67). *Tr.*

4.   Emmanuel Mounier (1905-1950) was the founder of the personalist movement and the journal *Esprit*. *Tr.*